Best wishes for the future.

V. A. V Carr.

Victor"

CAGE AND AVIARY SERIES

CAGE BIRD
HYBRIDS

Other Books Available

The Pheasants of the World
Dr. Jean Delacour

The Gloster Fancy Canary
John S. Cross

Poultry Colour Guide
Dr. J. Batty and Charles Francis

Ornamental Waterfowl
A.A. Johnson and W.H. Payn

Exhibition and Flying Pigeons
Harry G. Wheeler

Guide to Cage Birds
David Alderton

The Peafowl of the World
Josef Bergmann

The Yorkshire Canary
Ernest Howson

Pheasants and their Enemies
Dr. J. O'C. Fitzsimons

Domesticated Ducks and Geese
Dr. J. Batty

CAGE BIRD
HYBRIDS

By

V. A. V. Carr

With Colour Plates by
Michael Stringer

SECOND EDITION

Published by

SAIGA PUBLISHING CO. LTD.,
1 Royal Parade, Hindhead, Surrey
GU26 6TD   England.

To my father, Percy Carr.

© V.A.V. CARR and SAIGA PUBLISHING, 1980
ISBN 0 904558 81 9

SECOND EDITION

First Edition published as *Mule and Hybrid Birds*
for *Cage Birds*

Typeset by Ebony Typesetting, Cornwall in 12pt Baskerville

Printed and bound in Great Britain
by Billing and Sons Limited and Kemp Hall Bindery
Guildford, London, Oxford, Worcester

Published by:
SAIGA PUBLISHING CO. LTD.
1 Royal Parade, Hindhead, Surrey,

CONTENTS

MONOCHROME ILLUSTRATIONS

COLOURED ILLUSTRATIONS

viii

ACKNOWLEDGEMENTS

I would like to express my gratitude to the following persons and organisations for their invaluable help in completing this book: *Cage and Aviary Birds* for supplying many of the necessary photographs; Dr. T.G. Taylor, M.A., for the information on feeding and foods; and, finally, the Royal Society for the Protection of Birds for allowing us to reproduce important information concerning cage birds and the law.

My thanks is also extended to all photographers whose work has been used within the following pages, among them:

Barling Studios
E.V. Breeze Jones,
M.K.V. Carr,
Harry V. Lacey,
Frank Martin, and
Frank W. Orme.

V.A.V. Carr

FOREWORD TO THE FIRST EDITION

During recent years there has been increasing interest shown in the breeding of our native birds in cage and aviary, and more has been learned of their breeding and feeding habits during this period than ever before.

This has resulted in a renewed enthusiasm for the production of mules and hybrids; these can be exciting birds to breed, difficult certainly, but with great possibilities of satisfactory achievement and even profit — for good birds always demand good prices.

The younger generation of fanciers have a better basic knowledge of British birds by virtue of lessons learned at school, the continuation of instruction by radio broadcasts and the wide range of up-to-date books available at our national libraries.

Victor Carr's new book is timely, for younger breeders have felt the need of a book written in the light of recent experience. Here is a book written for them by a young man who has great knowledge and experience on the subject of breeding all British birds, mules and hybrids, for, being a son of the famous breeder and exhibitor, Percy Carr, he has, since childhood, hardly had a moment away from the care of aviaries and birdrooms.

As a boy he would stand quietly watching birds of other fanciers and listening to the teaching of his elders. He would learn and read all he could and add it to his personal experiences. He has through the years attended to the feeding and breeding of all species of British birds and hybrids — many of them rare — with great success. Always willing to help others, he learned to write on the subject and to lecture, and many fanciers, old and young, have profited by his instruction.

One sometimes hears it said that learning is not enough and that what is needed is experience. The fact is that neither is enough in itself. None of us lives long enough to learn by experience alone and the younger generations know this to be true, hence their willingness to learn.

This book shows that Knowledge plus Experience equals Success.

Hylton Blythe, F.Z.S.

Frontispiece 1 **Cock Goldfinch x Canary Mule.**
(Courtesy: Cage and Aviary Birds, photo courtesy: Harry V Lacey)

xii

Frontispiece 2 **Canary x Bullfinch.**

(Courtesy: Cage and Aviary Birds, photo courtesy: E.V. Breeze Jones)

xiii

INTRODUCTION

My dictionary's definition of a hybrid reads: "offspring of two animals or plants of different species or varieties or families". For mule: "offspring of a cross between canary and other finch". No doubt because of the challenge, these definitions have led to an interest in the breeding of mules and hybrids, and this hobby has a remarkable hold on a very large number of people. Why this should be is difficult to explain. A perfect example of a rare cross seems to stimulate those who have not been able to produce such a thing, and they are determined to "have a go", while those who have been successful once, twice or even three times like to go on and on.

That such crosses are sterile, and not capable of reproducing themselves does not slow down the annual enthusiasm to breed more and more. However, the fact that they are difficult to produce, compared with straight crosses, may be the clue to this enthusiasm, as man is always trying to conquer something or someone, somehow!

The only known and proved non-sterile mule is a cross between the Hooded Siskin and Canary. The fertility of this parentage led to attempts, by enthusiasts, to produce a red Canary using the red factor of the Hooded Siskin as a base for the colour gene. After some forty years of breeding some success is being achieved up to a red/orange *Standard*.

Something else I am unable to explain is the cash value

of such crosses. Even a normal insignificant mule or hybrid attracts a sale, so in his peculiar "kink" the would-be breeder is emulated by the purchaser who wishes to own a bird that is neither one thing nor the other.

Needless to say, the value of a perfect exhibition species is high, and the rarer and more perfect it is, the greater the value. It is obvious, therefore, that in this commercial world, for such a value to prevail, the demand must exceed the supply, and this has been so for as long as I can remember.

I mention all this to underline the fact that hybrid breeding and the production of the perfect mule have their great disappointments, but when successful they are wholly gratifying. There is no doubt that the organisation of shows by cage bird societies throughout the British Isles, catering (among others) for mules and hybrids, has certainly helped to popularise these birds. More often than not the supreme award for the best bird in show goes to a good and rare hybrid, and as such prizes are usually valuable, the purchase price of the bird can be viewed in the light of the awards likely to be gained during a period of, say, six to seven years.

It is perfectly true that many aviculturists breed certain mules and hybrids accidentally in so much as it was not a planned exercise. The sexes were correct and youngsters were produced. Nearly always, these examples are discovered by alert fanciers and, consequently, find their way into the exhibition world for many to enjoy or even criticise.

Another important factor that comes into hybrid breeding nowadays is the fact that for many years bird breeding has been carried out with great success, and many fanciers, whether interested in hybridizing or not, breed many of our native species in cage and aviary. It should be possible, therefore, after many generations of controlled breeding to produce a more domesticated type of British bird for crossing than was possible in the past.

I do not lay this down as a hard and fast rule, but suggest that the knowledge gained from producing such birds and using them to produce something else is more than half-way to the ultimate goal. The more confidence the parent birds have in their handlers the less likely they are to commit indiscretions associated with birds that regard their attendant as an intruder and not as a very interested helper in all they are trying to do.

Before 1933, British birds could be purchased from personal selections in pet shops and also bought, begged or borrowed from private individuals. As a result of the Protection Acts, however, the sale of any bird in the British list is prohibited, with the exception of aviary-bred speci-mens wearing a close-fitting ring, fixed on the bird's leg while still small and in the nest. (See Chapter 19.)

In recent years *Bird Protection Acts* have been amended allowing wild birds to be taken under licence for avicultural purposes. These licences can be obtained from the Department of the Environment, Bristol. Sympathetic consideration is given to applicants who wish to build up or retain their stocks, as it is appreciated that losses always occur. This is helpful for those practising straight British bird breeding.

So, for more than twenty years the quantity of birds available to would-be purchasers has been extremely limited, and, naturally, not many breeders of British birds are anxious to sell their young stock. As yet there is nobody who has undertaken the breeding of British birds entirely as a commercial proposition, and I look forward to the day when some enterprising person will branch out in this way.

So much for the stock with which you intend to start. The next important consideration is the housing of these birds for reproduction. There are many schools of thought on this subject, and the types of mules or hybrids one is intending to breed must be considered. The Light (or Clear), the Evenly Marked and the Self Dark are the three standards in the mule section, while for hybrids there is the normal or the dark specimen showing distinct characteristic parents, with size and shape being the important points for which to breed.

For mule breeding the large breeding cage is sufficient, housed in a light, vermin proof birdroom of even temperature. Occasionally, even some hybrids have been produced in these conditions, but not very often. The cage should be large enough to house one pair of potential mulers, giving them plenty of space.

The outdoor aviary is the best structure for hybrid breeding, varying in size from 3 feet wide, 6 feet high and 6 feet deep. The width can be varied to 4, 5 or even 7 feet, the height and depth remaining the same. I am confident that the best results will be achieved from a single pair housed in a 6 feet x 6 feet x 6 feet compartment, preferably of all wire construction, with a second layer of wire netting at least 2 inches away from the original to ward off cats, hawks, owls, etc.

A vermin proof floor, either of concrete, small mesh wire netting or bricks, would be a long-term advantage to avoid any accidents in the future.

Bird keepers must be aware of the law referring to the protection of some of the species mentioned in this book when they exist in their wild state. For this reason an additional chapter has been added

which summarizes the current position.

Unless otherwise stated, the assumption throughout this book is that the birds concerned have been bred in captivity.

METRICATION TABLE

Inches		Centimetres	Feet		Metres
1	=	2.54	1	=	0.305
2	=	5.08	2	=	0.610
3	=	7.62	3	=	0.914
4	=	10.16	4	=	1.219
5	=	12.70	5	=	1.524
6	=	15.24	6	=	1.829
7	=	17.78	7	=	2.134
8	=	20.32	8	=	2.438
9	=	22.86	9	=	2.743

Ounces		Grammes	Pounds		Kilo-grammes
1	=	28.350	1	=	0.454
2	=	56.699	2	=	0.907
3	=	85.048	3	=	1.361
4	=	113.398	4	=	1.814
5	=	141.748	5	=	2.268
6	=	170.097	6	=	2.722
7	=	198.446	7	=	3.175
8	=	226.796	8	=	3.629
9	=	255.146	9	=	4.082

1
Light Mules

Figure 1.1 **Norwich Canary** — often used in the breeding of mules.

1

LIGHT MULES

The term mule is very loosely applied, and it usually refers to the offspring of a Canary and some other bird. The aim of most aviculturists is to produce a bird that is as clear as a Clear Canary and as large as a good Norwich, showing its parentage without much doubt.

Years ago, before the controlled breeding of different coloured British birds, i.e. albinos, lutinos, fawns, etc., the appearance of a Light mule was purely accidental. Accidental that is, in so far as the "clear production" gene was not considered in the first instance. If a pair proved themselves capable of breeding in this way their value in succeeding years as potential breeders of further Clear mules was evident, but such pairs have always been very rare indeed.

Using finch type parent birds that are colour carriers makes the task of Light mule breeding much more of a certainty. Years ago some attempt was made to produce a strain of Canaries so in-bred that their capability of breeding very pale buff birds was certain. These were hatched from the pairing of two yellows whose ancestry was already known.

The in-bred Canaries were always called "sib. bred", the name given to related stock, no doubt from the word "siblings" which means brothers and sisters. Recent breedings, however, point to the cock bird as being

3

responsible for the capability of his offspring to be canary plumaged rather than having his own red/brown colouration.

Quite a few Greenfinch mules are now produced from a lutino carrier cock or a lutino Greenfinch cock paired to a hen Canary. Moreover, because the lutino coloured Greenfinch is bred under control in captivity it is available for mule breeding in this context. Up to this moment in time I do not know of any other lutino British species which is freely bred.

I must again emphasize that until a normal coloured pair have proved themselves, it is not possible to set out on a deliberate policy of producing a light mule. The

Figure 1.2 **A Light Mule**
An artist's impression of a rare Light Mule — the Linnet Mule. The dark feathers have spoilt the perfection, but a breeder of such a bird would be very proud.
(Taken from a painting by R.A. Voles)

4

introduction of a colour factor in one of the parents (or both), which must have some known pedigree, involving, therefore, a deliberately pursued policy, can have results. Generally the results could be the expected ones, but the raw material, as it were, with which to work is almost non-existent.

If anyone sees anywhere a rare coloured bird that could be used to produce a new coloured finch and then a new coloured mule, an attempt should be made to inform somebody who may be able to take advantage of this most precious "raw" material.

Figure 2.1 **Canary x Bullfinch**
(*Photo Courtesy:* M.K.V. Carr)

2
Dark Mules

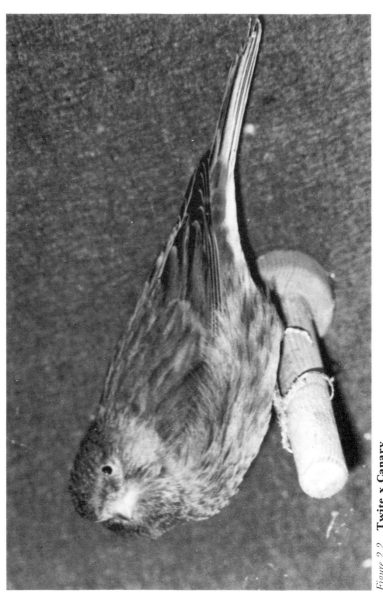

Figure 2.2 **Twite x Canary**
The cock Twite makes an attentive parent but this mule is not often seen on the show bench.
(*Photo courtesy:* M.K.V. Carr)

2

DARK MULES

Dark mules are the most common coloured Canary hybrids that are bred, some for exhibition and some for the quality of their song. The Goldfinch mule is doubtless the most popular, as it is catered for in the exhibition world in both normal and miniature sized birds. There is no doubt that the song of the Goldfinch, heard through the beak of the Goldfinch mule, is unsurpassed. The Linnet cross is another favourite for its song.

When in prime breeding condition the Goldfinch loses its black mark on the tip of the beak, this being quite clear. This occurs any time from March onward, depending on how late or early the spring sunshine may be. On the other hand, when the vigorous Linnet is in condition, its beak turns from a sickly looking grey or light colour to a deep, glossy black. Its plumage will have deepened in tone of colour all over, and will be very glossy.

The Greenfinch mule is perhaps the easiest to breed and rear. The largest type of Canary with the largest type of Greenfinch should produce the best form of mule. The Greenfinch is one of the most common of our native birds, and is becoming increasingly popular, no doubt because it is easy to keep, becomes tame and is quite a colourful specimen.

The Siskin comes next in popularity as a muler. It makes the tamest of pets, the most devoted of parents and has a versatile taste in foods. This mule is a particularly smart and engaging cross to try to breed. There is, in fact, no smarter looking canary hybrid than a tight-feathered, stout, cone-shaped, distinctly marked and deep level-coloured Yellow Siskin mule.

The Redpoll mule is a perky bird, not so handsome or so gorgeous in plumage as some of its brethren, but its sombre appearance and smart active ways make it quite a favourite. Size, as usual, is the aim, using as large and shapely a Canary hen as possible.

The Twite Canary has many similarities to the Linnet Canary, and father Twite makes a very attentive parent.

All the above varieties have been produced in quantities down the ages. The Bramblefinch and all varieties of Buntings have not sired successfully with the hen Canary (or, for that matter, *vice versa*), and anyone who is the first to produce any of these will make a name for himself in the annals of bird fanciers. Recently the first mule bred from a cock Canary and hen Chaffinch was produced. This created much interest; its parentage was easy to recognise but, unfortunately, it was a hen bird. I would imagine that a cock mule from this parentage would be interesting to speculate upon.

Similarly, one example of a Crossbill and a Canary has been produced in recent years and this cross created a great deal of interest as it opened up the possibility of using the Crossbill for further hybridisation; i.e. mated to a Greenfinch. The Sparrow, both House and Tree, one would think capable of fertilizing the hen Canary, but so far as I know this has not yet been achieved.

10

TYPES TO BREED

In all the different varieties of mules, the good big yellow bird is the ideal to attempt. The good big buff bird is also very useful, but when competing in a show with the yellow of equal size, it has, naturally, to take second place. I do not belittle the good buff, as in larger shows it is catered for in a separate class, in which case the competition of its yellow cousin is eliminated.

The term "yellow" is difficult to explain, inasmuch as the word is not to be taken literally. Most varieties of birds are divided into two forms, "Yellows" and "Buffs", whether a Goldfinch, Blackbird, or Chaffinch, etc., is concerned. The description can divide every species into two separate colour types.

A buff bird has a mealyness about the feathers or a greyish tint superimposed on top of the basic colour. A yellow has no such tint superimposed. The basic colour shines in all its natural state. It is almost like comparing green fields in the distance on a day of very clear visibility with the same view when a heat haze hangs delicately over the whole scene.

Yellow and Buff Goldfinch mules are very obvious, and this also applies to Yellow and Buff Siskin and Greenfinch mules, as the yellow and green in these birds is "hazed" over. Linnet mules are a better colour than the parent bird, while Twite mules show distinctive variations.

Although George Bernard Shaw's saying — "The Golden Rule is — there are no golden rules", should always be borne in mind, one very simple rule is that to have any real chance of success in producing an exhibition Dark mule you must use hens of *Norwich type*, but not necessarily pure Norwich. At one of the National Shows

11

the winning dark buff Goldfinch mule was bred from a *yellow* Norwich x Yorkshire hen, and a few years before that its brother also won at the National.

Generally speaking, it is always advisable to use yellow hens. Variegated hen Canaries are probably the best to use for Goldfinch and Linnet males because one is less likely to get mismarked mules, that is, birds with an odd light feather about them, which spoils a good Dark mule for exhibition purposes.

Regarding Siskin and Greenfinch mules, the chance of breeding mismarked mules is much less likely, consequently you can use clear and lightly marked Canaries, with an excellent chance of producing a good Dark mule. You usually produce better dark buff mules from yellow hens than by using buff hens. They are usually so much richer in colour.

So by always using yellow hens for muling you stand a chance of producing yellow mules and good buffs. It is usually best to *delay your mule breeding until May at the earliest*. This is most important, as experience has shown.

The best plan is to run your finches with their respective Canary mates through February and March. When April arrives the Canaries will want to go to nest, but the chances are that the male finches are not in breeding condition as early as April. Do not, therefore, let the hens lay infertile clutches of eggs, but remove their mates for the time being and introduce cock Canaries.

Each hen Canary should go to nest and lay its clutch of eggs which have been fertilized by the cock Canary. When she is nicely settled, remove the cock Canary and reintroduce the finch. It is usually best to use a dividing wire slide in the breeding cage, leaving the finch in the one compartment for safety's sake, just in case he should interfere with the eggs.

12

Figure 2.3 **Dark Greenfinch Mule**
(Courtesy: Cage and Aviary Birds, photo courtesy: E.V. Breeze Jones)

13

Figure 2.4 **Dark Linnet Mule**
       (Courtesy: Cage and Aviary Birds, photo courtesy: E.V. Breeze Jones)

KEEP PAIRS TOGETHER

When the hen Canary hatches, leave the finch with her all the time; he may help to feed the young Canaries. During this period the finch is coming more forward, and by the time the hen is ready to lay her second clutch he should be fit to fertilize her eggs.

It is most important to shut off the finch each night when the hen Canary is going to lay the following morning, because there is always a chance he may peck the precious egg. As soon as the egg is removed from the nest, and replaced with a dummy, let the finch return to the hen and remain with her all day until the evening when he should be shut off again. When the hen Canary has completed her clutch, replace all her eggs and shut off the finch.

So far as feeding the hen is concerned, when young mules are being reared, generally speaking, you should follow the same lines as for rearing Canaries. Always study your hens as individuals and watch their likes and dislikes. Greenfoods such as forms of seeding weeds are most essential.

Mules usually grow much faster than Canaries and if well fed are very often out of the nest at fourteen days old. I always think it is best to let the hen Canary feed her young as long as possible, and only remove them when she starts to incubate again. You will, of course, have reintroduced the finch as soon as the young mules hatch — i.e., a day or two after hatching. When young mules are removed from their parents it is advisable to keep them in large cages so that they can get ample exercise, which assists them to develop.

Colour feed birds either by using tasteless red pepper or a proprietary brand of colouring agent named carophyll;

both are extensively used. The red pepper can either be purchased ready-mixed for feeding or one can mix it with egg food or the normal seed mixture which is offered every day. To make sure the red pepper is absorbed into the bird's system it is imperative that the whole mixture is slightly moistened. Without the addition of a moistener the red pepper does not adhere to the food and will be left uneaten in the receptacle. If feeding is done daily in small quantities, water can be used as the moistener. For longer periods of time, and to ensure no mould is created, olive oil or a cooking oil can be used as a moistener.

Carophyll can also be used mixed with the foods previously mentioned or, more conveniently, can be used in the drinking water. The amounts to be used should tend towards too little rather than too much, as an excess of a colour agent can spoil the bird's appearance. Some fanciers resent the use of colour feeding, their argument being that it is not natural, but there is no doubt in my mind that if you can bring out the best of colour shades, why not? The aim should always be to produce the best, wherever possible, using methods that comply with proven acceptable standards of behaviour.

The easiest method of preparing the carophyll is to mix one teaspoonful with a cupful of boiling water so that the solids are completely dissolved. Add further water to this solution to fill a pint bottle. This is the approximate strength to use for drinking water and the drinking utensil can be topped up as and when required. This same solution can be used to moisten the egg food or other soft food provided. When this method of colour feeding is employed, there is no need to use a colour agent in the normal seed diet.

Always allow young mules to bathe freely, and if at all

possible supply them with soft water; it makes a wonderful difference to the quality of the feather.

Young mules should be trained to get accustomed to their exhibition cages. Run the birds into them whenever you can just for a short time. It is surprising how they soon get accustomed to them.

CLASSES AT SHOWS

Since the last war a greater interest has been taken in the breeding of mules and hybrids. It would be a grand sight to see full classes of mules at a show. If more mules were bred, we could have separate classes for the different varieties at our open shows, so please do all you can to persuade fanciers interested in this most fascinating branch of the hobby to put up as many muling pairs as possible.

There are many reasons why it is best to delay mule breeding until mid-May or June. For instance, if you try to produce mules early, the hen lays and sits on an infertile clutch of eggs; and she will not sit much longer than fourteen days. She finishes incubating and then wants to go to nest again, but this is still too early, and the result is another clear round. In this way two clutches have been wasted.

By delaying breeding operations, or rather by running a cock Canary with the hen, as I have already suggested, securing good eggs and, we hope, young ones, the breeding cycle takes a normal course. After rearing young the hen is in a natural condition to produce more fertile eggs.

Redpoll and Twite mules are seen less on the show bench than any other mules. I think this is a pity, and I do wish fanciers would try more for these crosses. Yellow hens should always be used, of any variety. If Mealy Redpolls

17

are available the extra size would help in producing a nice cobby type of mule.

Goldfinch x Canary

When cock Goldfinches are in full breeding condition their beaks go completely clear, losing the small black stripe they carry through the winter months. Introduce the cock Goldfinch to a hen Canary and also a cock Canary as well. As the hen Canary is usually ready to start breeding sooner than the Goldfinch she will pair with the cock Canary and hopefully have young. The presence of the cock Goldfinch should not prove too much of a distraction at this stage and he will be interested in his new surroundings and getting to know his future new partner.

When the hen Canary has completed her nest and is ready for laying, remove the cock Goldfinch where he can observe but not interfere. A wire slide to fit part of the breeding cage is the best method for separation. After the hen Canary has laid her complete clutch of eggs, remove the cock Canary. It is hoped that the eggs have been fertilized and when they hatch out reintroduce the cock Goldfinch. He should be interested and may help feed the young. Sometimes cock Goldfinches will peck the eggs in the nest, thereby destroying them, so it is essential that he is not reintroduced until this stage has been passed.

If all goes well and the hen Canary successfully rears her brood and they then leave the nest, the Goldfinch should be in forward enough condition to be capable of breeding himself. However, the young Canaries should be left as they are until they can fend for themselves. This will become apparent as they will cease calling out for food and get on with acquiring their dietary requirements themselves. Your Goldfinch cock should now go to nest with the Canary but as soon as the first egg is laid the finch should be removed to avoid any damage which he may be blamed for. This separation is preferably done overnight. The Canary's egg should be carefully removed and replaced by a dummy egg and the cock Goldfinch reintroduced the following day. This process should be repeated; the finch removed and the second egg replaced with a dummy. When the full clutch has been laid, replace all the eggs in the nest, take away the dummies and keep father away. The incubation period is about thirteen days and as soon as hatching out has been completed the cock bird may be reintroduced.

Linnet x Canary

The same procedure described for the Goldfinch can be followed in breeding this cross. The cock Linnet does not have the same reputation for interfering as the Goldfinch, so there is no need to remove him when egg laying is being undertaken by the hen.

Greenfinch x Canary

The cock Greenfinch is not such a reliable hybridiser as other finches, but using the hen Greenfinch with a cock Canary has proved to be a far more reliable method of achieving this mule. The hen Greenfinch makes an excellent feeder of youngsters and is generally very reliable in all aspects of motherhood. No problems exist with this mating as previously described for the Goldfinch and the young offspring are healthy and not prone to the enteritis virus which breeders of pure Greenfinches often experience in their birds.

19

Siskin x Canary
The Siskin is a very popular bird with most fanciers. It is closely related to the Goldfinch in its feeding and general behaviour — active, inquisitive, somewhat greedy but can become fascinatingly tame and confiding. In spite of its small stature, when in prime condition this bird can fertilize any size of Canary. To avoid any disappointments treat the Siskin cock with the same caution as described for the Goldfinch.

Twite x Canary
The cock Twite becomes a very attached father to the canary and young of his choice. This attachment can cause problems at the nest as he likes helping in the construction and carries building material about a lot. Do not trust the Twite, therefore, when the eggs are being produced.

Redpoll x Canary
This is not a common bird within the mule family. The Redpoll is very difficult to sex but when you have a cock in good breeding condition he will let everybody know. They are always worth trying and pose no problem if you have fertile birds.

I have mentioned all the favoured or commoner Canary hybrids. Others that have been produced in authentic isolation are Crossbill x Canary (1964) and Canary x Chaffinch (1974).

These birds were interesting from every aspect of achievement and one's own mental picture of the desired progeny was either proved right or wrong, according to one's expectations. The Crossbill x Canary was bred in a large cage and some hand feeding was necessary to help the young bird survive the first few days. The Crossbill itself is a lovely cage bird, once mature, with great personality.

Figure 2.5 **Siskin x Canary** — a popular mule due to its tameness and smart appearance. (*Photo courtesy:* M.K.V. Carr)

3
Mules for Song

Figure 3.1 **The 'Schoolmaster' Songster** — the Goldfinch has an attractive song and may be used to teach other birds.

(*Photo courtesy*: M.K.V. Carr)

3

MULES FOR SONG

In the preceding chapters we have been considering chiefly the production and management of mules primarily intended for the show bench, but there are bound to be many specimens bred that are useless for this purpose, because, even with the greatest care in mating any kind of livestock, the show specimens bred are invariably in the minority.

Many of the "wastrels" are quite handsome and make attractive pet song birds. As such they command a ready sale if cock birds are in vigorous song, and they cannot altogether be accounted a loss.

In the usual conditions in which a pet bird is kept a cock mule makes a much more suitable pet than the conventional little yellow bird, the Canary, as it is much hardier, longer-lived, and more varied in colour. Its song, too, is not so ear-piercing, and is freely uttered throughout the year, sometimes even during the moult.

A few years' experience will enable the fancier to pick out from among the youngsters of the year those specimens that will be likely to turn out suitable for the show bench.

It is difficult to convey this knowledge in writing, as there are really no hard-and-fast rules to go by, although, generally speaking, the largest birds, when of fairly good colour, will be the most likely to develop into exhibition specimens.

Still, one must not be in too great a hurry to discard a bird if on the small side, as smallish birds are nearly always jonques, few of these equalling the buffs in size, even when full grown. Type and carriage are natural points that are not observable to the inexperienced, and frequently not even to the practised eye at this early stage.

Those youngsters, however, which you feel convinced will never make show birds should be turned into a flight cage when fully fledged, then place near to them, in a cage, a "schoolmaster" songster of some kind — a mule, Canary, Goldfinch, Linnet, or trained Bullfinch, or whatever kind of song bird you wish them to copy.

The bird or birds used must, of course, be free songsters, and the young birds, no matter what their parentage, will copy practically any song within reason. It would be unreasonable, of course, to expect them to repeat in its entirety a very full and lengthy song like that of the Skylark or Nightingale. But there is no reason why a short vigorous lay like that of the Chaffinch should not be learnt if a free singing schoolmaster of this species is procurable.

A TUTOR NEEDED

It is desirable that the birds should have a tutor of some kind if intended for singing purposes, for if simply left to their own devices they will pick up what they happen to hear, and it may be utter rubbish so far as song is concerned, such as the call-note of a hen Canary, or the chirrup of a Sparrow, or they may fail to sing at all if isolated from other singing birds while still immature.

If it is possible to keep both pupils and tutor in a room separate from other birds, it will conduce greatly to the clearness of the final song that is learned. If they are kept in the breeding room there is the likelihood that they will imitate other birds besides their teacher, and the purity of their song will thus be spoilt. In my opinion, any of the songs mentioned above is preferable to the song of the Canary, unless it is a well trained Roller, and naturally schoolmasters of this breed are expensive.

The song of either the Goldfinch or Linnet sounds exceedingly pretty, and not in the least offensive to the most sensitive ear. All mules learn either of these ditties with ease. Birds, too, which sing their song (whatever it is) perfectly, without mixing up other songs with it, are worth a few more pence than poor songsters.

When the young birds are from ten to twelve weeks old they will commence to warble, but they cannot really be said to sing until after they have completed their moult and reached the next summer.

It is seldom that one is able to arrange for a schoolmaster to sing to them during the whole time that the moult is in progress, unless the tutor itself has been forced to moult unnaturally early in the year, say, in May or June. However, in ordinary circumstances, they will again hear the, now familiar, strains when they finish moulting. It is then that the good work done before the moult will begin to bear fruit, the song heard by the young birds while still in their nest feathering having really been memorized by them at that time.

One might liken the receptive faculties of all young things to a blank gramophone disc — open to receive whatever impression is brought into contact with it. These impressions lie dormant until called into being by, in the one case memory, typified by the voice of the tutor, and in the other the needle of the gramophone.

When they have finished moulting, the young cock mules should be caged singly in box or song cages so that there may be nothing to distract their attention from perfecting their song.

4
Bullfinch Hybrids

Figure 4.1 **Bullfinch** — one of the most popular of our native finches.

4

BULLFINCH HYBRIDS

The Bullfinch is one of the most popular Finches of our native shores, being noted for its colour and unusual "piping" song. The cock bird has never been used with success when hybridizing. Why, I do not know, but for all that it is worthy of trial.

In the spring and summer months it is disastrous to house more than one cock in a cage or aviary, as they get very pugnacious and jealous when in breeding condition. This condition is long lived as they can start early in the spring and carry on through until the late summer.

Hens can also fall out among themselves, but not quite as pugnaciously as the males, so it is expedient to house these birds out of contact with their own species. Their unfriendliness is confined only to their own breed, generally speaking, but very rarely they may make assaults on other species, in which case your own observation will enable you to remedy any ills that may befall the victims.

The nests are constructed rather characteristically with a fairly large base of wiry twigs on which the nest is built of sisal, hair, etc. The string basket and wicker cage are favoured and also nest pans, Hartz Roller Canary cages, etc.

They lay from as few as three eggs up to as many as seven of a greenish-blue ground colour with some purple-brown markings. The incubation period is twelve days.

31

Their food varies from buds in the spring to berries of rowan, privet, etc., in the autumn, but hemp and sunflower can be their main stock mixture. Niger and canary seed are also taken, but the provision of any other seeds is immaterial and they could be wasted.

Soft food, and also live food of as varied a selection as is obtainable at the appropriate time of year, is necessary for rearing, and the seeding heads of dandelions, grass seeds, sow thistle, shepherds purse, plantain, etc., help considerably for successful results.

Any youngster bred from the Bullfinch is of a characteristic colour, and sexing is nearly impossible until the moult has commenced. When only a few new breast feathers have appeared, however, one's hopes or fears can then be put to rest.

For a very long time the Bullfinch hybrid has been the most coveted to produce, whether using the Goldfinch, Linnet, Canary, Redpoll or Greenfinch as the male.

The male Bullfinch mated to a Goldfinch, Linnet, Canary, etc., has never produced any authenticated offspring. Many theories have been advanced to prove that the cock Bullfinch is incapable of mating with any other species of bird. Whether true or not, these theories have not been proved wrong, and I should like someone to disprove them by producing a hybrid with a cock Bullfinch.

The most common of these hybrids is doubtless the Goldfinch x Bullfinch, as it is easier for a Goldfinch to be attracted to any mate than it is for any other finches. The Greenfinch x Bullfinch comes next, followed by the Linnet, Canary and finally the Redpoll. The Siskin x Bullfinch has been claimed once, to my knowledge, but the specimen was imperfect in many ways. Doubtless it was a hen bird, and in consequence most uninteresting from a colour point of view.

Some Goldfinch x Bullfinches have too much black in their blaze, cheeks, etc. The mediocre types of Linnet x Bullfinches are too dark and lack the red or orange tint associated with the perfect specimen. The perfect specimen is one's ideal, of course, but is not always produced quite so easily.

Greenfinch x Bullfinch hybrids (cock birds) are similar in many respects to the Canary x Bullfinch, but lack the distinct "pencil" marks running down the back. The yellow or "jonque" Canary x Bullfinch, as opposed to the buff, has these "pencil" marks less pronounced.

The hen Canary x Bullfinch hybrid is the most colourful of the hen hybrids, and is quite attractive. The remaining hen hybrids of the foregoing species are not colourful compared with the cocks, and have little value in comparison with them. The cock birds, on the other hand, are nice to look at, especially if they have the perfect colour, marking and "yellow" plumage.

Up to 1887 only five Canary x Bullfinch hybrids had been proved as established identities, and since then many have been produced. In 1957 only one was reared, as far as I could find out; in 1958 I knew of five whilst in 1978 nine Canary x Bullfinch hybrids were reported as having been bred over the whole of the British Isles, so readers will have some idea of the vagaries involved. Very many Canary x Bullfinch hybrid pairs must be attempted each year, and the percentage of successful matings is very low.

USE LARGE CAGES

Cages and aviaries are used for successful propagation, and I would advise the use of the largest possible cage but not too large an aviary. Good, big, yellow cock Canaries make the best parents from the point of view of colour and size. Young cock Canaries, having no experience with their own species, perhaps make better mates for the Bullfinch, but this is a point one does not like to be too dogmatic about. On rare occasions one gets cock birds that take no notice of any species of hen, in which case they are best eliminated as potential breeders.

The pure self colour is the more desirable, the larger the bird the better, provided it is healthy, virile and not lazy. I have seen good results from green cocks, but self-coloured birds throw purer youngsters with not too many foul markings.

The keeping of potential breeders together over the winter months saves a period of introduction in the spring and summer, and the tame, confiding types are always the more reliable. It is always advisable to see that there is no aggressive intention between parent birds when in the breeding season, as fatal results can occur. If any pro-longed aggression exists, it is best to separate the offending pair and consider another mating.

A wild or restless bird (and we all know that such temperaments exist in all types of livestock) does not make a good parent in an aviary, but birds that are tame and used to all their natural enemies such as cats, dogs and even humans, do not communicate such instincts to their mates and offspring.

Birds that have out-of-season moults are never in their right "breeding" condition and should be avoided.

Goldfinch x Bullfinch
This bird, I should say, is the most commonly produced of all the Bullfinch hybrids. It is the favourite, partly because

34

Figure 4.2 **Goldfinch x Bullfinch Hybrid**
(*Courtesy: Cage and Aviary Birds, photo courtesy: Frank Martin*)

35

the Goldfinch is so popular and partly because many fanciers like to keep a hen Bullfinch for hybridizing.

The number of hen Bullfinches used throughout the British Isles must be very great. The number of eggs laid by these Bullfinches could swell the funds of the Egg Marketing Board (if they were saleable). The number of actual fertile eggs . . . well, that is another story!

The colourful characteristics of this hybrid can be expected knowing how bright both parents are in the male form. The Bullfinch's ability to pass on this colour to its offspring is no doubt the reason why it is so popular, but I think other finches, although not producing such colourful youngsters, do not cause so many dashed hopes after optimistic anticipation.

I mention this so that readers are not lulled by a false sense of security to put this pair together and then sit back and wait for results. You are going "agin" Nature, remember, and that is no light task to take on.

When the cock Goldfinch is in breeding condition it loses the black streak in the upper mandible, which appears pure white, while the white cheeks become whiter. He "proud tails" very frequently, and if he has amorous intentions towards his mate, will demonstrate them in an obvious manner by following the chosen hen from place to place almost all the time until they are like substance and shadow.

If, on the other hand, there are other inmates in the enclosure, more often than not he adopts most aggressive intentions to the rival, whether it be male or female. Unless speedy action is taken to remove this rival some harm is sure to result.

The time of year that this particular pair choose to contemplate raising a family varies according to conditions prevailing in the winter and also the temperature during the spring months. If they are housed during the winter in warm, artificially lit surroundings and the sun shines a lot in March and April, they are ready much earlier than if they are kept in less favourable conditions. Artificial light certainly has a stimulating effect on egg production.

If the hybridizing pair are housed under fully natural conditions, as governed by the sun, then one has to wait until the sun is of sufficient warmth and duration to stimulate the ovaries and other sexual organs to get them into the state that is termed "breeding condition".

I have known Goldfinch x Bullfinches hatched in early April on the one hand and not until September on the other. One can only hazard the guess that their development in April was assisted by their winter quarters, while with the September birds most of the summer months were spent in getting up to the necessary condition.

Linnet x Bullfinch
This is a satisfactory hybrid to produce and the type can vary considerably. I have seen some very good coloured birds, and also some a lot darker in the plumage, and therefore not appearing to be so good.

Linnets' intentions, when they are keen on their hens, are obvious, and usually this is a good guide. Again, be careful that no aggressive attacks are made on any other inmates of the aviary.

The male's wedding garb is denoted by a heightening of colour in his plumage, and the beak will become black and highly polished.

Redpoll x Bullfinch
This cross has not been in existence more than a hundred

years at the very most. In fact, many hybrids have been produced for the first time since then, and I find this rather surprising because I always imagined our forefathers were keener naturalists than we of the past two decades, but I suppose, on thinking it over, there were fewer opportunities, a smaller population, other interests and little chance of passing on information.

This hybrid is the smallest of the Bullfinch range and very distinctive in its garb, showing its parentage in no uncertain manner.

Some use the large Mealy Redpoll as the sire in order, physically, to compete with the hen Bullfinch. Others use the smaller Lesser species with a small hen Bullfinch for the same reason. It is superfluous to say, from the point of view of exhibiting, that the larger the progeny the better — but a little one is better than none at all!

The difficulty in producing these hybrids is to find a Redpoll you are certain is a cock bird, and I know of no physical determination.

There must be very many Redpolls that are not cock birds housed with hen Bullfinches, and what a frightful waste of time is involved. The surest way of knowing one has a cock bird is when you see him flying around a tremendous amount uttering his piercing shrill "trill" — in fact, "trilling" a great deal of his time. Those of you who have had this problem of sexing Redpolls will appreciate that a cock bird when in keen breeding condition is unmistakable by his noisy antics.

Redpolls are naturally very "pally" and will make a fuss of any bird that is willing to be fussed over. They make good parents in their feeding methods, and it is, perhaps, surprising, in view of their amorous intentions and their attentiveness to their mates, that the hybrid is not more

Figure 4.3 **Cock Linnet x Bullfinch Hybrid.**
This bird shows the typical perching position of this hybrid.
(Courtesy: Cage and Aviary Birds, photo courtesy: E.V. Breeze Jones)

39

numerous. Perhaps the difficulty of sex definition accounts for most of the disappointments.

Greenfinch x Bullfinch
This is another popular hybrid. The Greenfinch is a great favourite among British bird fanciers, no doubt because of the ease with which it can be catered for and its high degree of domestication. They breed prolifically, make excellent feeders and parents, and are anxious to get on with their nesting operations during the whole summer.

In size and colour there are vast differences — small yellows, large buffs, large yellows, mediocre buffs, and so on. The large yellow — and he is yellow in every sense — is the perfect specimen, and in size and temperament very close to the Bullfinch. The yellow certainly gives a better implantation of colour in his hybrids, thereby enhancing their values.

Nothing comes amiss in the way of food — an important factor in hybrid rearing as opposed to breeding — and apart from being a cheerful aviary inmate it is very easy to determine whether the Greenfinch is in breeding condition.

This hybrid is very close to the Canary x Bullfinch in colour and, perhaps, size, if the parents are of the same stature. One distinction the Greenfinch x Bullfinch pair have is their willingess for mating. It is perhaps surprising that, in spite of this, the success of this behaviour viewed in the light of fertility in the eggs is very disappointing, and I have come to the conclusion that the more modest, secretive habits that one knows nothing about can reap the most successful harvest. Perhaps there is a moral in this!

Possibilities
We have not seen the Twite, Siskin, Crossbill or Hawfinch as possible sires of the hen Bullfinch. Whether the Chaffinch or Bramblefinch could be encouraged to fertilize the hen Bullfinch remains something which a future generation must achieve.

Figure 4.4 **Greenfinch x Bullfinch** — very similar to the Bullfinch Mule in colour and size.
(Photo courtesy: M.K.V. Carr)

5
Goldfinch Hybrids

Figure 5.1 **Goldfinch.**
The most colourful of finches with its crimson-marked head and yellow wing bar.

5

GOLDFINCH HYBRIDS

The most colourful and popular of our native finches is the Goldfinch, which is easily recognized by the crimson, white and black of the head and the bright yellow bar on the wing. Wings, tails and quills are black with white on the tip.

The hen is distinguished by a less conspicuous expanse of colour. The cheeks are brownish-white and the wing butts, when outstretched, are brownish-black compared with the cock bird's jet black wing butts.

Another feature are the nostril feathers or "hair". In the cock they are black, while the hen's are greyish.

These birds usually cause some difficulty in sexing, especially if the hen is an exceptionally good one in every respect, but the distinguishing features described are always accurate in one way or another.

When in breeding condition the black streak running down the beak (in both sexes) disappears, the beak then being pure white. The descriptive remark associated with these birds; i.e. "proud tailing", is always a pointer to good forward condition. This "proud tailing" is shown by the bird swinging its body from side to side, with the tail in a rigid position following the body, and at the same time emitting a short burst of song or call.

Their nesting habits are reliable as a rule, but sometimes the cock (whose affection for his mate is obvious during the whole of the time they are paired) can be mischievous and do damage to the eggs when the incubating hen is away, but if sufficient interest is provided by means of outside attraction this action, which I consider the result of boredom, can be avoided.

I have described in detail in the Goldfinch x Canary section how to avoid the interference of the cock Goldfinch when using a cage for their breeding quarters. An aviary of larger dimensions does not usually require such close control over the Goldfinch's freedom of movement as he can find other forms of distraction.

The nest is very neatly built with bents, moss, roots and lichen, and lined with down, wool and hairs. The eggs, usually four to five in number, are of a bluish-white ground colour with a few streaks and spots of purplish-brown. The incubation period is twelve days.

Their stock seed can consist of niger seed alone, but the usual mixture of niger, hemp and canary seed is the safest to give them. There is no need to offer any other kind. When rearing young, live food is not much sought after, but if they are used to eating cut-up mealworms, ants' eggs, etc., so much the better.

It is advisable to provide soft food, and the seeding heads of dandelions, chickweed, groundsel, and all varieties of thistles may be included during the summer months.

Youngsters bred from the Goldfinch are of a distinctive plumage, the final colour coming out in full after their first moult.

The Bullfinch hybrids mentioned in the previous chapter all relate to those bred from the hen Bullfinch and cock birds of other species. In this chapter I shall mention hybrids bred from the Goldfinch only where the bird takes its place as the sire. I have refrained from mentioning

46

hybrids in reverse, namely, using the hen Goldfinch and cock birds of other species, as the hen Goldfinch will be mentioned in succeeding chapters with her respective mates, thereby avoiding any duplication.

Goldfinch x Greenfinch

The most common hybrid is the Goldfinch x Greenfinch. It looks just what it is, a tighter, larger type of Greenfinch, with a red blaze and goldish-yellowish wing bars.

These two birds are about the readiest to hybridize. Greenfinches, as most fanciers are aware, breed very freely in confinement, while the male Goldfinch is usually looking for a mate when not in contact with his own kith and kin. What is easier, then, than this state of affairs for a beginning?

The cock Goldfinch can perhaps be very inquisitive when sitting is in progress, sometimes interfering with the eggs with his large beak, in which case they may get broken. But this is not a frequent occurrence when the surroundings are large enough for the curiosity of this bird to be devoted to other matters.

A large specimen of this hybrid usually does well in exhibition circles, but has unfortunately to take second place if any good Bullfinch hybrids are in competition. However, I am sure that if plenty of these birds were produced, special classes would be provided at most of the shows instead of, as at present, at only the larger ones.

Goldfinch x Linnet

This is another easy one to breed as the Linnet is another of what one might loosely term "domesticated types". It is this high degree of domestication that makes the difference between ease and difficulty of breeding — whether pure or

47

crosses.

The colour and marking of this hybrid are again what one would expect, a more colourful Linnet in every way with the distinguishing Goldfinch blaze in obvious outline.

From the point of view of song they are high on the list, but for competition I should say they would take second place to the Goldfinch x Greenfinch.

Goldfinch x Twite

As the Twite is also known by the name "Mountain Linnet", the close resemblance to its "cousin" is reflected in this hybrid. The latter is very similar in detail to the Linnet with the exception of its beak; the Twite's short, yellowish beak being one of the distinguishing features.

Goldfinch x Siskin

This bird is one of the liveliest to produce. It does not show as much colour as the previously mentioned hybrids, but both the Goldfinch and Siskin are very popular as aviary inmates and the hybrid carries something of the characters of the parents.

The Goldfinch and Siskin are closely related in the grouping of families so the possibilities of satisfactory results are not too surprising.

Siskins are fond of live food when rearing and it is essential that they have access to some. This is perhaps one difficulty in production, but it is the only one, everything else being as for the other varieties.

The live food problem will be dealt with in the chapter devoted to foods and rearing, but I should mention in passing that housing the Goldfinch with the Siskin is ideal from the point of view of feeding as their habits in this respect are identical. This, however, does not apply to their rearing habits.

Figure 5.2 **Bullfinch and Goldfinch Mules.**
Top: Goldfinch x Canary, *Bottom:* Canary x Bullfinch. *(Courtesy: Cage and Aviary Birds,* taken from a painting by R.A. Voles)

49

Goldfinch x Redpoll
This cross came automatically to mind after discussing the previous one. It is a very pretty hybrid, and from the colour angle is the next favourite, assuming Bullfinch hybrids get all the honours for colour.

Its rich bright colours contrast beautifully on a small shapely body. It inherits the smart jaunty action of the Redpoll, and shows off as much as any Goldfinch.

The feeding habits of the parents are identical, and they will nest very readily. The vexed question of sexing Redpolls, previously referred to, comes into the picture again, but as hens seem to predominate the chances are more than likely that your Redpoll will be a hen.

Goldfinch x Chaffinch
It is pleasing to mention this cross as the first one I have ever seen was bred in 1958 by Mr. R. Tout of Portsmouth. Others may have been produced in the early part of the twentieth century, but they were never recorded as having been bred prior to the end of the nineteenth century.

This bird was produced simply by housing a cock Goldfinch with other hen finches. As it was obviously in very forward condition, which coincided with the Chaffinch being in her best reproductive mood, a successful mating took place with one youngster resulting.

It is interesting to record that another inmate of the aviary (a hen Bullfinch) captured the Goldfinch's attention, and he forsook his true love. Fortunately, a cock Bramblefinch "married" the hen Chaffinch for her next round, and a nest of Bramblefinch x Chaffinch resulted.

This coinciding of breeding condition in both sexes is no doubt the secret of successful breeding, especially with the very rare crosses.

This Goldfinch x Chaffinch hybrid showed its parentage very well. The white wing bars always associated with the Chaffinch showed a yellowish type; the head and beak were typical of what one might expect and altogether it made an interesting comparison with many past conjectures of what to expect.

The second Goldfinch x Chaffinch hybrid was bred by my father in July 1959. One fertile egg hatched out in early July from a pair that had had two clear rounds of nests before, eight eggs in all. This third nest contained four eggs, only one of which was fertile.

There was no prior evidence of these birds being the slightest bit interested in one another, until a youngster was noticed in the nest five days old, during which time it had been effectively fed by the hen Chaffinch with egg food and live ants' eggs.

The aviary was 6 feet x 6 feet x 6 feet with only the one pair housed together since March. The Goldfinch was two years old, the Chaffinch six years, and they were not introduced to each other before March. Neither bird had had any previous nesting experience to show any results.

Goldfinch x Bramblefinch

This has been claimed only once to my knowledge, but the fact that the Goldfinch x Chaffinch has proved successful makes this a certainty in the future. The methods of housing, feeding etc. are the same as those employed for the Chaffinch.

There are no other species of British birds that one can speculate upon for successful mating with the cock Goldfinch with any hope of successful results. Perhaps the Goldfinch x Sparrow could be a speculation, in which case one can include the Bunting family as well, but the possibility of any "familiarity" between these species is very remote.

6
Chaffinch Hybrids

Figure 6.1 **Chaffinch** — an early nester.

6

CHAFFINCH HYBRIDS

One of the most common of our British finches is the Chaffinch, and it should be one of the most popular. It is one of our earliest nesters and significantly enough, although only single brooded in the wild state, will have four or five nests in confinement, regularly and trustworthily.

The male bird undergoes a radical change of plumage when in breeding condition. The crown is slate-blue and also the nape. The mantle is chestnut-brown, the rump greenish, and the throat and breast brown. The beak is very dark blue.

This colour change or "exaggeration" takes place gradually through the late winter months, reaching completion in late March or early April. Some birds come into colour sooner than this, and their singing capabilities when in condition are very impressive.

The hen is very dull, a yellowish-brown or whitish-brown predominating in the body colour. All the offspring resemble the hen and any hybrids bred are not sexed with absolute certainty until after their first moult.

Most immature hen Chaffinches are noticeably smaller than the cock birds and the same distinction is noticeable in young hybrids. After the first moult a light brown chest and flanks are noticed, compared to the ashy-grey of the hen Chaffinch.

The nest is very neat and compact, built at varying heights of grasses, moss, roots, wool, etc. The whole thing is woven together in some degree and externally decorated with lichen or even paper. The nest is lined with hair and/or feathers.

Invariably Chaffinches can be very finicky (see Chapter on "Management") in their selection of a nesting site and are fussy in their building operations. It will be found by experience that wicker or sisal baskets when chosen by the hen save a lot of preparatory work in "foundation laying". Furthermore, the roughness of these containers permits the builder to do a bit of weaving or interlacing of the materials on hand. Short lengths of sisal and small tufts of cotton wool are the two materials that will attract most birds.

Eggs are greenish or brownish stone colour with spots and streaks of dark purple-brown. The incubation period is ten to eleven days.

Their feeding habits are inexpensive and varied. All seeds of the brassica family, hemp, niger, and canary seed, make a good stock mixture. When rearing young, live food and soft food are essential, as Chaffinches are very much like Softbills during this time, right up to the period that regurgitation commences, which happens any time after the youngsters are a week or more old.

The only hybrid produced so far from the cock Chaffinch is by mating this bird to the hen Bramblefinch. This is not surprising, as they are almost of the same family and congregate together, roosting and feeding, in the autumn and winter months.

As the Bramblefinch leaves these islands in April and early May, returning to the continent (Scandinavia, Finland, etc.), its association with the Chaffinch is interrupted for a while. Whether there is any communal life with the

Light Goldfinch
Mule

Siskin
Mule

...amon
...eenfinch
...e

...anary x
...ullfinch
Mule ♂

Twite
Mule

...ino
...enfinch
...e

Dark
Linnet
Mule

Dark
Goldfinch
Mule

·M·STRINGER·

Plate 1   Mules

continental Chaffinch, I do not know.

The hybrid is interesting for its colour and markings, and some are quite difficult to separate from the true Brambling. In hen finch classes I have seen hen Bramble x Chaffinch hybrids inadvertently entered and accepted as hen Bramblings by the judge.

I mention this to emphasize the final result of this particular mating. It is a frequent product these days, and something one feels quite proud about, but the real good ones are not so numerous.

Plenty of natural food is necessary for the parents. In fact, the Bramblefinch is wholly insectivorous for the first week or so when feeding young. This desire for live food can be very disturbing for a watchful owner as he will observe the Bramblefinch flying all over the aviary looking here, there and everywhere and at the same time uttering a most unusual breeding note of alarm.

I always feel, when watching these antics, that the young ones are being starved of food and also of heat as the hen should be spending more of her time brooding instead of making fruitless efforts to find whatever she is searching for. This requirement has to be satisfied, and the provision of live ants' eggs helps for a while until the parent appears to get tired of them and starts looking all over again. Small gentles help, well scoured; also the gentle chrysalis when in not too "ripe" a condition. Earwigs are favourites, while moth pupæ, cut up, or small mealworms, spiders, green grubs, moths, caterpillars, etc., may also be used.

It is always expedient to remember that Chaffinches are early nesters and, when in confinement, remain in breeding condition for a long time, so early pairing is advisable. The cock Chaffinch undergoes a very remarkable colour change in the spring. All his body

57

feathers alter appreciably, the head is a deep blue, the beak a very dark blue, while the chest colours are much improved and the wing whites very pronounced.

There has never been any definite proof of a hybrid being produced from the Chaffinch x hen Greenfinch mating. In reverse, of course, they are fairly plentiful, but one always assumes them to be Greenfinch x hen Chaffinch.

The possibilities of breeding the Chaffinch x Bullfinch, Chaffinch x Linnet, Chaffinch x Redpoll, Chaffinch x Siskin, Chaffinch x Twite, Chaffinch x Canary, Chaffinch x Goldfinch (already referred to in reverse when discussing the Goldfinch hybrids) and finally the Chaffinch x all species of Buntings, are immense, and we look forward to the day when any of these are produced, backed by impartial evidence.

7
Bramblefinch
Hybrids

Figure 7.1 **Bramblefinch** — a colourful winter visitor to these islands.

7

BRAMBLEFINCH HYBRIDS

The Bramblefinch is a favourite with many fanciers, but not very popular with others. As it is a winter visitor to these islands, returning to the continent and the Baltic States in the spring, it has two periodical fits of restlessness, calling out in the night for several nights, and tending to upset other inmates. This restlessness does not last too long, fortunately, and they make good parents when this migratory fever has passed.

The cock is a colourful bird with a bright chestnut throat and breast. The feathers of the head and mantle are blue-black when in breeding condition; otherwise these head feathers are edged ruddy brown. The underparts of the breast and vent are white.

The hen is of a less distinctive colour, namely, brownish-grey with mottled brownish feathers on head and mantle.

The nest is bulkier than that of the Chaffinch, but similarly constructed with the same apparent attempt to weave slightly when constructing. The wicker or string basket, Hartz Canary cage, bushes, etc., are easily taken to, and nesting materials consist of grasses, bents, and sisal, with hair, feathers, or cotton wool for lining. The eggs, five, six, or seven, are darker than those of the Chaffinch and are greener, although similarly marked. The incubation period is nine to ten days, and I think this one of the shortest periods of any of our native birds.

Their stock feeding is not an expensive item, as they will thrive on rape, charlock or other brassica seeds, linseed, ground or soaked barley and rolled wheat. Hemp, canary, niger and sunflowers are also relished. In fact, the Bramblefinch is an easy bird for which to cater. It has a melodious song when in the breeding season, and makes many peculiar notes that one does not hear at any other time of the year.

For rearing purposes, live food is essential, also soft food and soaked seed to take the place of seeding heads of wild foods, as I know of no seeding heads that this bird favours. The live food should be in the main ants' eggs, with gentles, mealworms, moth pupæ, etc., as a second and necessary choice.

Cock Bramblefinches can become quite aggressive when they are thinking of choosing their mates, and it is advisable when it is evident that pairing is taking place to remove any other aviary inmates that may become victims of such aggression.

MOST COMMON CROSS

The most common hybrid, of course, with this bird is the Bramblefinch x Chaffinch. All the remarks made in connection with the Chaffinch x Bramblefinch apply in this case, including the reference to livefood and fads.

The hybrids from both crosses are almost identical, and it is only the smaller amount of white on the wing bars and the slightly smaller head of the Bramblefinch that give some clue to the male parent. But even these distinctions are not infallible, and one needs great experience to be able to hazard a reasonably correct guess, let alone a definite

Figure 7.2 **Bramblefinch x Chaffinch Hybrid.**
In this case a cock Chaffinch was used but the reverse cross would be very similar and, more often than not, difficult to differentiate. The parentage is obvious, however, in either case. *(Courtesy: Cage and Aviary Birds, photo courtesy:* E.V. Breeze Jones)

answer, whether the hybrid in question is a Bramblefinch x Chaffinch or a Chaffinch x Bramblefinch.

Similar remarks to those made concerning the Chaffinch apply to the Bramblefinch when speculating on other crosses, and the range of new hybrids that could be bred is as considerable.

The Bramblefinch x Greenfinch is a distinct possibility as it has been produced in reverse (see Greenfinch hybrids). Another possibility is the Bramblefinch x Bullfinch. Frequent matings have been observed between these birds, but no fertile eggs were produced. This may not be the fault of the Bramblefinch — one cannot tell.

The Bramblefinch crossed with the Linnet, the Twite, the Siskin, the Redpoll, the Canary, all species of Bunting, and the Goldfinch, all come under the category of something new! So there is plenty of scope for the enthusiast.

8

Greenfinch
Hybrids

Figure 8.1 **Greenfinch** — the most common of our aviary birds and one which is easily domesticated.

8
GREENFINCH HYBRIDS

Greenfinches are the most common of our aviary birds, and certainly the most domesticated in respect of breeding and pairing. There is a wide range of colour among both sexes of these birds.

Yellows and buffs are very obvious, but in the main the plumage is yellowish-green, with bright yellow primaries and base of tail. The back when in breeding condition assumes a darker hue, sometimes an almost purplish-blue.

The hen is duller with a browner head and mantle. The young ones are striped with brown. The sexing of these youngsters is obvious, the cock showing the more colour.

Greenfinches will nest in colonies and often two or three cocks can be placed with five or six hens of different species, provided the aviary enclosure is large enough. They make good parents and their pairings and courtship are obvious.

They will nest in almost any circumstance, building quite the most substantial structure of any of our finches. It is built of twigs and moss with bits of wool, sisal and bents, and lined with bents, sisal, hair, feathers and/or cotton wool. The eggs, usually four to six in number, are of a pale purplish-white or pale greenish with a few red spots and streaks. The incubation period is thirteen days and many broods can be expected in the season.

Evidence of the breeding condition can be seen in the song that this produces, and also the active movements and challenging attitudes of the males.

The weakness in these birds that is becoming increasingly prevalent is in their eyes. An infection becomes obvious, leaving a distinctive watery ring around the eye, and if treatment is not effective blindness can result.

This ailment could be due to a mineral deficiency, and the administering of several drops of cod-liver oil into the mouth leaves a miserable mess that will not be cleared until a moult has replaced the old feathers, but it will cure the complaint.

Their feeding habits are spread over a wide range, varying from cereals, i.e. wheat, barley, oats and canary seed to charlock, linseed, rape, hemp and sunflower seeds. For rearing purposes live food is not essential, but it is a great advantage if the bird is interested in or educated to take whatever is offered of this type of food.

Seeding heads of wild seeds of the dandelion, groundsel, chickweed and sow thistle type meet their other needs. Regurgitated kernels of dry seed have not the same quickly assimilated value of these seeding or soaked seeds as they are not yet fully hardened and ripened. Soft food is readily taken, and is essential.

Young Greenfinches are very problematical birds. Sometimes for unaccountable reasons they will gradually fade away at about eight weeks old, even although able to do very well for themselves in respect of feeding, etc.

Enteritis is one of the diseases to which they are subject and the use of some of the sulpha drugs in the drinking water has some retarding effect on this disease, but much research work is required before the causes of this ailment are known.

"Diairol" has been found to be a useful chemical to add

to the drinking water. This ailment is not, however, in evidence in respect of any mules or hybrids bred with the Greenfinch.

Mr. A.H. Scott, the well known breeder of lutino Greenfinches, is of the opinion that they tend to be less strong than normals. As these birds can be used for the production of Light mules they are very useful inasmuch as their products are valuable, although sterile.

The Greenfinch makes an excellent foster mother for Canaries, Bullfinches, etc; for any bird, in fact, that is not likely to require a quantity of live food.

Greenfinch x Goldfinch
This takes pride of place, naturally, and has already been referred to when discussing the mating in reverse.

All things being equal, it is fairly sure of successful results. Cock Greenfinches assist in the feeding of their babies, and if you place other species of hens (no more than two) in the same aviary he can be husband to both in their turn during the summer months.

The favourite alternative is, of course, the hen Chaffinch (as mentioned in an earlier chapter), and with the Goldfinch, which is a little later coming into condition, as the second string to your bow, you would have the ideal pairings.

Obviously it is a little disconcerting if one has ambitions to produce a Greenfinch x Chaffinch hybrid, and then the Goldfinch takes the Greenfinch's attention from the start. Then you will have to decide whether to remove the Goldfinch, the Chaffinch, or leave well alone, hoping that your original plans will shape into some reality.

Greenfinch x Chaffinch

This is a comparatively new hybrid, and one that is now bred fairly regularly. By that I do not mean to imply it is common — far from it. It is not colourful, even in the male sex, as the green or yellow of the Greenfinch predominates; a factor from the colour angle common to all these green birds when mated to such a colourful specimen as the Chaffinch.

Why this should be I cannot attempt to explain, but it is a great disappointment that such colours cannot be brought to predominance. The Chaffinch is an early and regular nester in captivity, and when provided with live food and soft food she makes a good feeder. The hybrid is larger than its mother, and shows its parentage well in both sexes.

Greenfinch x Siskin

A very pleasing hybrid with quite a remarkable quality of feather, so close and silky in texture fitted on to a perfectly formed body, with the parentage obviously displayed. The massive head, neck and shoulders of the Greenfinch are coupled with the full broad chest, thereby securing for it the description of "waggon horse" for size and type.

The hen Siskin makes a wonderful mother, encouraged by green food and live food. As they are naturally tame, their nesting operations from building to rearing are quite delightful to watch in all stages. I cannot understand why more of this cross are not produced.

Figure 8.2 **Greenfinch x Chaffinch Hybrid.**
This bird shows the bold appearance of the Greenfinch. The
characteristic Chaffinch wing bars are pronounced but the body
colour of the Chaffinch is missing, as the green of the Greenfinch
predominates.
(Courtesy: Cage and Aviary Birds, photo courtesy: Barling Studios*)*

71

Greenfinch x Redpoll

Not a pretty hybrid, looking more like a large, cumbersome Redpoll with all its finer points outweighed by the Greenfinch.

A trace of the bib can be seen and the markings are less artistic, but the characteristic jauntiness of the Redpoll is obvious.

Greenfinch x Linnet

Resembles the Greenfinch x Redpoll in some ways, but shows more of the "lines" of the Linnet. A faint trace of the Greenfinch's colour can be seen down most of the front.

Greenfinch x Twite

This is another of the same pattern as the foregoing and is easy to breed. Twites of either sex are sensible birds to have in aviaries, and make excellent parents. What a difference this does make.

The hybrids are not colourful at all, and are robust and blustering rather like the Greenfinch. They have not the pleasant "hovering" attitude of the Twite.

Greenfinch x Bramblefinch

This has been produced only a very few times. The only one I have seen was a hen bird, and there was no difficulty in deciding on the parentage.

I should imagine the cock hybrid could be quite unusual, and it is definitely well worth while trying to produce it. I have known several pairs to be tried, the Greenfinches following their hens in a typical Greenfinch manner, assisting in the nesting operations and doing everything except produce fertile eggs.

72

Redpoll x
Bullfinch

Goldfinch x
Greenfinch

Greenfinch
x Bullfinch

Goldfinch
x Redpoll

Linnet x
Bullfinch

Brambling
x Chaffinch

Goldfinch
x Bullfinch

Greenfinch
x Chaffinch

·M·STRINGER·

Plate 2   Hybrids

Greenfinch x Crossbill
This hybrid has not been produced using the cock Greenfinch as the sire. It is, however, a likely hybrid to produce if a cock Crossbill is mated with a hen Greenfinch; this cross has been produced by several breeders in recent years. Having a Greenfinch as one of the parents means that feeding of the young should not be too difficult.

So much for the Greenfinch hybrids. Possibilities are not very numerous. A favourite so often tried, but never produced, is the Greenfinch x Hawfinch, most fanciers using as small a hen Hawfinch as possible. I have heard of many of these pairs feeding one another, but apart from this chumminess nothing else happened.

One could add the Greenfinch x Yellow, Cirl or Reed Buntings, but no Bunting on the British list has yet crossed with another finch.

Figure 8.3 **Redpoll x Greenfinch** — a less colourful hybrid than others produced from Greenfinch matings.

(Photo courtesy: M.K.V. Carr*)*

9
Siskin Hybrids

Figure 9.1 **Siskin** — live food is essential for the rearing of these birds.

9

SISKIN HYBRIDS

The cock Siskin is recognised by its yellow and green plumage, black crown and bib and black flank markings. In captivity the bib, more often that not, is not very distinct, but when in breeding condition the cap and bib become very black. If no bib has been apparent, an outline of one will be seen when in tip-top condition.

The hen is greyer, with the head cap an olive-green with streaks, the chin dull white, and the flanks well marked. Young birds resemble their mother until after the first moult, but it will be noticed that the young cock birds have yellow outside tail feathers, which the hens never have.

The nests are beautifully constructed on a base of bunched twigs, wicker, wire or string baskets. The Hartz Roller Canary cage can also be used. The nest is built of small twigs, bents, sisal, moss or cotton wool, lined with down, hair or feathers. From three to six eggs are laid of a light blue coloration, with red-brown streaks or spots. The incubation period is eleven days. These birds are very fond of hemp, niger, canary and maw seed. They will thrive on any or all of these.

Siskins tend to eat a lot and get lazy and fat, but this can be cured by exercise. Live food is essential for rearing purposes, also soft food, which can be made up to almost any recipe as long as it contains some egg, milk and biscuit, etc. Both eggs and chopped mealworms are much relished,

Figure 9.2 **Siskin Mule**

The dam of this bird was a Norwich Canary.

(Courtesy: Cage and Aviary Birds, photo courtesy: Harry V. Lacey)

while chickweed, groundsel, dandelion and sow thistle are appreciated. It is always advantageous to give live ants' eggs.

As they are tame, domesticated and reliable as feeders, they make excellent foster mothers for almost all species of mules and hybrids for which help may be required.

The Siskin I consider to be the most domesticated of our native birds. It breeds freely among its own race in confinement, having several broods and plenty of young ones in each brood. I remember my father breeding twenty-three Greenfinch x Siskin hybrids from one pair in one season, and every youngster was sound and well. When such large families are produced much food is required.

Siskin hybrids consist of the Siskin x Goldfinch (referred to in the chapter on Goldfinch hybrids), Siskin x Greenfinch (referred to in the Greenfinch hybrid chapter) and the Siskin x Linnet. This last bird carries the distinctive markings of both parents. It is not colourful, the green or yellow of the Siskin being submerged by the brown or ash-grey of the Linnet, which is a great pity.

Siskin x Redpoll
This looks what it is and is very much a miniature product. I often wonder whether this hybrid could be fertile, as both parents are closely related. Is it safe to assume, therefore, that any progeny from this mating should be able to reproduce themselves? I wonder if anybody has tried?

As far as other possibilities are concerned, there has been no success with the hen Chaffinch, hen Bramblefinch, or hen Twite, to name but some. I think all are possible, and hope they will be tried, especially the first two.

Siskin x Chaffinch
A few isolated, fairly authentic reports have been received of successful hatching of Siskin x Chaffinch hybrids, but so far none of these has been reared to full maturity.

10
Redpoll Hybrids

Figure 10.1 **Mealy Redpoll** — this winter immigrant is larger than our native Lesser Redpoll but both are used in the breeding of hybrids.

10

REDPOLL HYBRIDS

Our resident race of Redpolls is of the small form commonly called the Lesser. There is a variation in size of this form and also in colour, but whatever type, sexing is difficult.

The larger Mealy Redpolls are immigrants to this country in the winter. Text books tell us that hens lack the pink rump and breast of the cock birds, but as this red colour usually disappears in confinement sexing is very difficult.

When in forward breeding condition the cock bird is very active, darting all over the place, hither and thither, uttering his very familiar *"chizzz. . . ."* which is very high pitched. The short bursts of song go something like *"chick-chick-chick-wee-wee"*.

I have known red breasted "cock" birds build nests and lay eggs; hence my emphasizing the difficulty of sexing.

The Redpoll nests readily in the wicker, wire or string baskets suitably provided with a firm base, preferably nestling in a small bunch of twigs, heather, or bunched evergreen such as box.

No height is required for construction purposes, and foundation should be provided in the form of small wiry twigs, coarse bents, or grass, sisal, etc., while for lining they will need cotton wool, hair and feathers. The eggs are usually four to six in number, the colour rather deep blue with some spots or streaks of brown. Incubation period is ten days.

Redpolls may be fed on niger and canary seed, while crushed hemp is appreciated. Soft food and live food should be provided, also sprouted seeds (those already mentioned) when rearing young. Chickweed, groundsel and sow thistle in their seeding stages are all beneficial.

Redpolls have been favourite birds with aviculturists for a very long time. Many fanciers must have seen them years ago kept in cages where they performed quite acrobatic displays to get their food and water. They had to pull a cord at the end of which rested a small receptacle with food and another with water. When they had had their fill these cords were released and dropped out of reach until they were needed again.

They are active, acrobatic feeders in their natural state, pulling the cones of the alder and the birch by their legs and beaks for easy extraction of the seeds.

For hybridizing, the larger the bird the better, but the sexing, as I have mentioned before, constitutes the major difficulty when selecting stock.

Hybrids already referred to when dealing with the reverse matings are: Redpoll x Greenfinch; Redpoll x Goldfinch; Redpoll x Linnet; Redpoll x Siskin, the Redpoll being the male in these crosses. When the Redpoll x Goldfinch is produced in this way it lacks the colour of the hybrid bred in the reverse mating.

Redpoll x Chaffinch
This has been produced only once to my knowledge, and that was in 1938 by my father. Unfortunately the bird died before it moulted out into adult plumage, but it shows every sign of being a hen. I say "shows" because it is now a

84

stuffed specimen in good order, revealing its parentage quite plainly — almost like a young hen Chaffinch with a bib.

I mention this as an inducement to others to try, and at the same time to include the Redpoll x Bramblefinch as a yet unknown possibility for the future.

Redpoll x Twite
Not a favourite amongst breeders as there is no colour interest, as one can imagine from such a mating.

Figure 10.2 **Redpoll x Goldfinch** — lacks the colour to be found in the offspring of the reverse mating. (*Photo courtesy:* M.K.V. Carr)

11
Linnet and Twite Hybrids

Figure 11.1   **Close Relations.**
     Top: Linnet
     Bottom: Twite

11

LINNET AND TWITE HYBRIDS

The Linnet is the largest of this group that also includes the Twite and the Redpoll. It is a popular aviary and cage bird and hybridizes readily. The male shows red on the crown and breast in its natural state; the hen none at all.

When aviary moulted the red features are replaced by a tinge of brown on the breast, and the chin and throat are whitish with streaks. When in breeding condition the beak changes from an ashy-grey to a highly polished black.

They build a substantial nest in bunches of heather, gorse or other bunches of twigs that may be supplied, provided there is an adequate base on which the foundation of the nest can be started. The Hartz Roller Canary wicker cage is favoured, also string or wooden baskets of not too large a size. They do not like nesting too high. For building materials they require grass, bents, short lengths of sisal, moss, a few twigs, and for lining purposes hair, wool (cotton) and feathers.

Usually four to six eggs are laid of a pale bluish-white in ground colour with a few spots and streaks of purplish-red. The incubation period is eleven days.

The favourite food of these birds is rape, charlock, canary and niger seed. Crushed hemp seed will be eaten, but their beak formation does not facilitate the easy cracking of this seed when whole.

When rearing young, sprouted seeds of any of the above,

89

with the addition of groundsel, chickweed and dandelion may be given. It is also advisable to give ants' eggs or other live food for a slight variation in the first few days after the youngsters have hatched and if the parent birds will take them, successful rearing usually results.

The singing capabilities of the Linnet are well known. Mules bred and kept in close proximity in order to learn this song from their parent are valuable as songsters.

Juvenile birds up to their first moult resemble the mother's drab colour, and the sexing of youngsters is difficult until after the moult.

Cock Linnets can usually be housed with more than one species of bird, certainly when in their winter quarters. In the breeding season, however, they should be watched in case they adopt a temporary aggressiveness to other aviary inmates. If this happens the victim should be removed. This "aggressiveness" should not be confused with the pairing habits, when the cock follows his chosen hen almost like a shadow. Really aggressive attacks with physical violence are meant.

Again, when considering hybridizing we are travelling on familiar ground inasmuch as most of the hybrids bred from the Linnet have already had judgement pronounced upon them when considering the mating in reverse. These include Goldfinch x Linnet, Greenfinch x Linnet, Siskin x Linnet, Redpoll x Linnet.

A Linnet x Twite hybrid was exhibited at Olympia in 1959, a jaunty bird with the distinctive characteristic of the Twite's beak showing but apart from that, nothing to recommend it.

Linnet x Bramblefinches have been hatched, but never reared to maturity. I hope this can be achieved in the not too distant future. As they have been hatched the most

90

likely contestant for similar honours must be the Linnet x Chaffinch, so "go to it" you first-time enthusiasts.

TWITE HYBRIDS

The Twite is a very close relative to the Linnet in many ways. It has a yellowish beak, which gets lighter in colour when in breeding condition. In natural surroundings the male has a red rump, but when in less natural conditions the red disappears, making it very difficult to sex these birds accurately.

The presence of white flights can sometimes indicate the cock bird, the hen having less predominant flights, but this distinction is not infallible. Youngsters are impossible to sex until their mature moult.

Twites are ready nesters in confinement, and make good, attentive parents requiring live food at rearing time. Their nests are built of bents or dead grasses with a few twigs, sisal, hair, etc., and are lined with wool or other softer material. Colourful eggs are laid of pale bluish- or yellowish-white with a few brown spots. The incubation period is eleven days. They are very fond of canary and niger seed. Hemp seed is taken if the kernel is not too hard, while rape and other brassica seeds are appreciated.

Twite hybrids have been previously mentioned when crossed in reverse with the Linnet. This bird represents, however, greater possibilities with new crosses than the Linnet. I know the Twite x Greenfinch and that is all. If this mating is possible, then surely the Twite x Bullfinch is possible; and if the Twite (or Mountain Linnet) with such close association to the Linnet cannot follow his first cousin in mating with birds the Linnet has chosen,

91

Figure 11.2 **Greenfinch x Twite Hybrid.**
This cross is not a colourful bird, but the parentage is obvious and
suggests that the Twite could be profitably employed with other
species of British birds.
(*Courtesy: Cage and Aviary Birds, photo courtesy:* Barling Studios)

there must be a wider gap in their so-called relationship than we imagine.

Twites need live food for rearing, such as ants' eggs, gentles, etc.

Figure 11.3 **Linnet Mule.**
(Photo courtesy: M.K.V. Carr)

12

Softbill or Insectivorous Forms

Figure 12.1 **The Mistle Thrush** — a popular and beautiful wild bird.

12

SOFTBILL OR INSECTIVOROUS FORMS

The Blackbird is an easy bird to sex, inasmuch as the cock is blacker in every way than the hen. When in breeding condition the Blackbird's beak turns completely yellow and the plumage has a greater gloss than when in its winter garb.

The Thrush is much more of a problem when sexing as there is no colour difference whatsoever. The song of the cock bird is quite proverbial, and this capacity for singing is some clear indication of where the sex lies. Another method is to "blow-up" feathers near the vent and usually in Thrushes there is evidence of a protrusion that indicates the cock which is obviously missing in the case of a female.

Both of these birds, i.e. Blackbird and Thrush, have identical tastes when nesting, feeding and rearing. They take to aviary accommodation very well and plenty of bush space, either natural or artificial, is used for the nesting site.

The nest is solidly built of grasses, twigs, roots and sometimes moss, solidified with dark earth or mud. The Blackbird lines its nest internally with dry grasses, while the Thrush's nest is lined with a very smooth layer of dung or mud or rotten wood, well maintained.

Both species eat soaked dog or puppy biscuits, meat meal, cooked potato, bread and milk; in fact, most household scraps, including fruit in the form of apples, pears, etc.

For rearing, a good supply of freshly acquired earthworms takes some beating, but the demand for these can be quite a problem. Gentles are appreciated and, of course, mealworms and ants' eggs.

Other insectivorous forms, of course, must also have gentles, mealworms and ants' eggs for rearing purposes, but the sooner any youngsters can be fed on an artificially made insectivorous mixture the better for the pocket, as the former feeding can be quite expensive. In any case this "meating off" on to this food from the more natural ones should not be delayed too long.

It is astonishing what a large amount of ripe or semi-rotten fruit Softbills will consume but it is usually cheap, especially if it has reached the stage of being unsaleable to the general public.

I shall not dwell too much on this subject of Softbill hybridization as up to the present time it has not been practised much, and it is of great importance that experience be gained with these birds as straight pairs, before attempting the unusual.

However, the suggestions I shall make are for those willing to experiment with the unusual. The Blackbird x Thrush has been bred on at least two occasions, and I well remember the first of these hybrids appearing on the show bench in the 1930s.

A SENSATION

The first public appearance of this bird caused quite a sensation, and as events turned out it was a great pity that this debut was not preceded by publication of all the breeding facts.

98

Figure 12.1 **Ring Ouzel x Mistle Thrush Hybrid.**
This hybrid, bred from two softbills, clearly shows its parentage.
(*Courtesy: Cage and Aviary Birds*)

99

It is extremely difficult for a judge when he is confronted with a bird, the like of which he has never seen or heard about. This bird to which I refer could have been quite correctly diagnosed as a melanistic Thrush, but on much closer examination it showed the parentage of the Blackbird. I see no difficulties in producing this hybrid, and am rather surprised that more have not been seen.

Another Softbill hybrid, produced in 1958, was the Yellow x Pied Wagtail, which was bred in an aviary, several youngsters being obtained from the one pair. As a hybrid, the parentage is far from being obvious, and the beautiful colours of the Yellow Wagtail have been superseded by those of the Pied.

Those of you who have the opportunity of seeing large flocks of Pied Wagtails in the country during the winter should have noticed the many variations in plumage. Age and locality count a little, while place of origin must give some explanation for a variation in colour. With all these variations the sudden emergence of a hybrid looking a bit like many of them certainly presents a problem.

However, Mr. J. Spinks, the breeder of this hybrid, had plenty of witnesses to his achievement, and it was well announced and accepted without doubts.

Fieldfare x Mistle Thrush
Fieldfare x Blackbird
These two hybrids were produced in 1978 for the first time and showed what may be achieved with persistent trying. Their parentages were apparent, otherwise their acceptance by the viewing public would not have been as enthusiastic had there been any doubt.

100

POSSIBLE EXPERIMENTS

There must be very many hybrids to be produced from a large number of Softbill species. The Robin x Nightingale has been tried by many with no success up to the present (1980). The Redstart should be considered with either the Robin or Nightingale or both. The Stonechat should cross with the Whinchat, Pipits should interbreed one with the other; the Fieldfare, Redwing, Ring Ouzel, Blackbird, Mistle and Song Thrushes are all possibilities for further hybridizing, one with another.

Indeed, these larger varieties when bred as straight pairs are easy to cater for in all their domestic and family requirements. Feeding does not constitute much of a problem with gentles, mealworms, ants' eggs, etc., freshly available.

This concludes the names of all the different mules and hybrids that have been bred. I have also indicated some very strong possibilities which I hope will soon become realities.

Figure 12.3 **Robin** — so far crosses including this bird have been unsuc-
cessful.

13
Suitable Aviaries

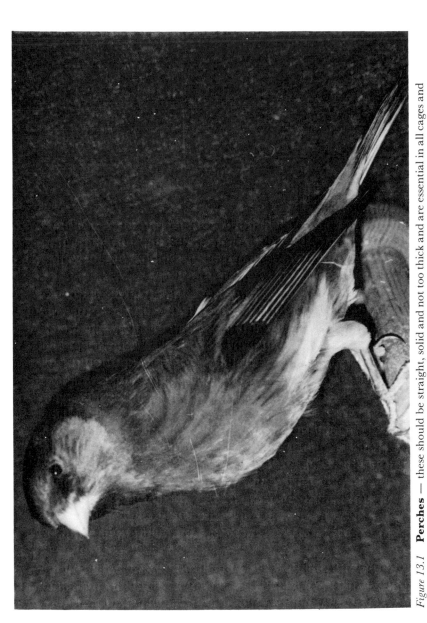

Figure 13.1 **Perches** — these should be straight, solid and not too thick and are essential in all cages and aviaries. Here we see a Goldfinch Mule on an ideal perch. (Photo courtesy: M.K.V. Carr)

13
SUITABLE AVIARIES

So far as accommodation is concerned, I hold very strong views on the sizes of aviaries. I know the average householder in this country has limited garden space, and what with the territorial claim of the woman of the house, the children and so forth, there is little left for father and his birds.

In the first place then, a birdroom with suitable large stock cages is an essential. With such a building the care and protection of your stock is nearly a hundred per cent secure during the months from September to March. Long, dark nights do not encourage good birdkeeping in aviaries when the weekend is the only time one has any daylight in which to see things.

The birdroom should be frostproof so that there is no problem about seeing that your birds are supplied with water that does not become solid ice.

On the other scale, the owner of spacious grounds for aviaries does not make use of his breeding aviaries for six to seven months of the year, and it is doubtful if many can lay out a considerable sum of money on buildings that are not in constant use. I know that the large, naturally planted aviary is ideal for housing birds in nearly perfectly natural conditions. However, it is not the ideal for breeding purposes, nor is it ideal for watching young birds. It is only ideal in a zoo or park.

105

Small aviaries in as natural a setting as is practicable have proved to be the best for breeding purposes. If one wishes, they can be made in sections, and dismantled for winter storage, but most sectional constructions cost more.

The size I am recommending is the now popular aviary, 6 feet x 6 feet x 6 feet single unit, of all-wire construction on an inexpensive 2 inches x 1 inch wooden batten frame. Half of the roof area should be covered by a frame on which glass or a glass substitute can be fixed.

No light is excluded when using this roofing material: a very important point. These single units can be built at home for the cost of 108 feet of 2 inches x 1 inch wooden battens, which means 16 pieces, 6 feet long, and about 12 feet for the construction of the door.

Use 3 feet wide wire netting of $\frac{1}{2}$-inch mesh running from the bottom of one side, over the roof and down to the bottom of the other side. This should be done twice, and where the edges of the wire meet a batten is used, (a) to strengthen framework of aviary; (b) to expedite the joining and fixing of the wire netting, and (c) to carry the frame on which the glass substitute or glass is fixed.

The diagram explains the construction in better detail.

MATERIALS REQUIRED

The specification of this aviary is as follows:

Approx. 16 yards of 3 feet wide $\frac{1}{2}$-inch mesh wire netting. 6 feet of 2 feet wide $\frac{1}{2}$-inch mesh wire netting for the front and door. 2 hinges, 2 door fasteners (1 inside, 1 outside). Roof to be all wire with half roof area covered glass or substitute, this frame to be constructed of tapered wood 8 inches high in middle, tapering to 1 inch outside on both sides.

Four boards all round the floor of the aviary $\frac{3}{4}$-inch thick, 14 inches high, 6 feet long. All wooden battens 2 inches x 1 inch including door. If there is more than one aviary, all doors to be the same height, opening inwards. The boards are partly buried in the ground to prevent wind blowing the aviary over. All battens to be nailed at inside corners of the boards to retain rigidity. Top roof battens overlap each other at corners; likewise boards. In actual fact therefore $\frac{3}{4}$ inch is lost in the overall length and breadth of the aviary.

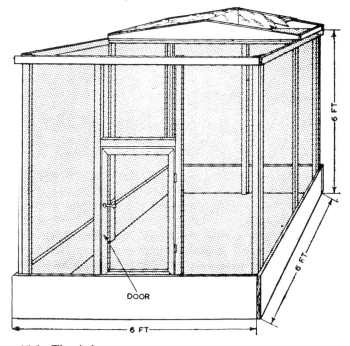

DOOR

6 FT

Figure 13.2   **The Aviary.**
The 6 feet x 6 feet unit described in this chapter is shown above. It is of all-wire construction and half the roof area is covered with a detachable frame of glass or a substitute material.

107

This method obviates the necessity for half jointing or other joints which hold moisture and cause rotting after a time. The front can be fitted with 2 feet wide wire.

Door approx. 2 feet wide.

This type of aviary is most suitable for not more than two pairs of birds. The intention, of course, must be to use it for only one pair in perfect breeding condition, but this happy state of affairs does not usually occur at the time the owner plans in his or her mind. To offset, as far as one is able, this lack of collaboration in respect of condition, and also the seasonal variation of condition in different species, two hen birds of early and late nesting habits can be chosen, housed with a cock bird of versatile breeding habits.

An example of this is a cock Greenfinch with a hen Chaffinch and a hen Bullfinch. Another example is a cock Goldfinch with a hen Siskin and a hen Bullfinch. These "pairings" can be "permutated" within reason, and experience, preferably recorded in diary over a period of several years, will show that this system can give the best results.

I know there is always the temptation to put as many pairs together as possible, especially in the halcyon days of spring. If you succumb to this temptation at least allow your better judgement to maintain an amount of flexibility during the course of the season, and re-move any inactive birds that could do harm to the active ones.

One hybrid pair and one pair of birds for straight breeding is also recommended, such as a Greenfinch x Chaffinch pair, housed with a straight pair of Siskins or even a pair of Canaries.

There are many other types and sizes of aviary, and your own personal facilities must decide your ultimate

108

SUITABLE AVIARIES

action. But the foregoing system is the one I most highly recommend.

Of course, the 6 feet x 6 feet x 6 feet can be varied in any of the measurements. The height is immaterial from the bird's point of view as there are very, very few aviary birds that fly up and down, like a helicopter. They prefer to fly from left to right parallel with the ground so the 6 feet width is essential as a minimum.

The 6 feet in height is used only as a personal convenience so that if one climbs in the aviary one can be in some comfort. There is nothing more tiring than stooping for any length of time with birds flying around one's knees.

The breadth could be reduced to 3 feet. In any case this measurement should be in any multiple of feet of the wire width you intend to use, e.g. one width of 3 feet wide mesh, two widths of 4 feet wire netting; or three of 2 feet to make in all 6 feet or two of 2 feet to make 4 feet.

Another important point is to have all the doors of the aviaries the same size in width and height, so that you are subconsciously aware of exactly how much room you have to clamber through. I have seen many old scars on bald heads because the bald head assumed his door was higher than it really was!

But whatever you do if you reduce the measurements, house only one pair. In terms of pairs of birds in a given cubic capacity however, you will find the 6 feet x 6 feet x 6 feet the most economical.

THE CORRIDOR TYPE

Another type of aviary is what is called the corridor type, which consists of a number of small aviaries in sections, built side by side, each section usually measuring 6 feet high, 6 feet long and 3 feet wide (or even 6 feet wide). The doors are in the front and right along the front of this range is a wide corridor which can be entered at either end, making it a huge safety door, as it were.

With a little planning this corridor can be used to transfer birds from one compartment to another without having to handle them. They simply fly from one aviary down the corridor to the one to which they are to be transferred.

The disadvantage of this corridor type of housing lies in the fact that all your muling or hybridising pairs are close together, within sight and sound of one another. More often than not, unless you can guarantee to have different species in the whole range, the cock of the species in one compartment will be courting at some distance the hen of the same species two, three or four compartments away, thereby reducing the chances of breeding with the hen properly provided.

This action, by the way, was encouraged some years ago when a cock bird was placed in a cage near to a hen of the same species in an aviary. The theory was that such a casual introduction would so excite the hen that the cock housed regularly with her would be encouraged to mate. More often than not, however, the reverse can occur — the hen could turn on this cock and have nothing whatever to do with him for the rest of the season.

Of course, this question of aviary size is an entirely individual matter and I do not think the aviary makes a lot of difference to results. But if one has a long term plan in mind it is easier and cheaper to standardize.

The ordinary common Canary breeding cage is often used by a large number of hybrid breeders. It is certainly

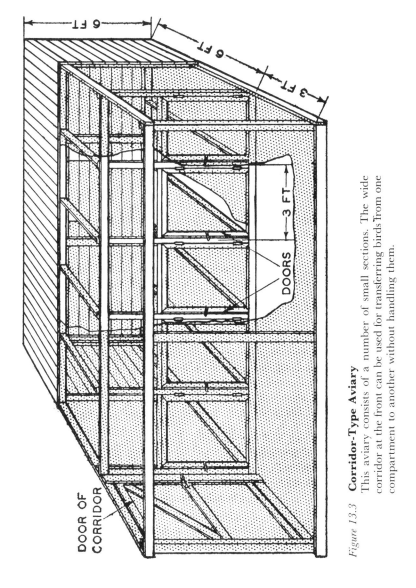

6 FT

6 FT

3 FT

3 FT

DOORS

DOOR OF
CORRIDOR

Figure 13.3 **Corridor-Type Aviary**
This aviary consists of a number of small sections. The wide corridor at the front can be used for transferring birds from one compartment to another without handling them.

111

extensively used for successful mule breeding. When incubation by the hen bird is taking place some fanciers keep the cock bird on its own by means of a slide; others put the male with another hen, hoping to make full use of him while in season.

CONDITIONS VARY

All these items are for individual action as conditions vary from room to room. If your birdroom is large enough, sections can be wired off from each other round the sides. I have seen the space between the lowest shelf and the actual floor of the birdroom wired into fairly large flights, with a wire top so that observation can be made without having to get on one's hands and knees to see what is going on.

The indoor aviary of whatever size has the advantage of being free from cats, owls, hawks, etc. A double layer of wire netting is essential for outdoor aviaries where cats, etc., are common. This second covering of wire need not be of $\frac{1}{2}$-inch mesh, and it need cover only half the roof and sides. It should be tacked on about 2 inches or so away from the inner netting.

Perch accommodation is an important consideration in all aviaries and cages. These should be straight and rigid, but not too thick, so that when mating takes place nothing that could be prevented occurs to upset an important part in the breeding programme.

14
Management

Figure 14.1 **Late Nester** — the Bullfinch.
(*Photo courtesy:* M.K.V. Carr)

14

MANAGEMENT

I am of the belief that the forwardness or otherwise of springtime bears more relationship with the moon than with our calendar. It is important, therefore, to have the birds already paired up in an early season, ready for the power of the sun to boost nature's reproduction in all its wonder and versatility.

There are always arguments on whether the weather has any effects on birds' breeding capabilities. I am sure it has. It affects the number of migrants coming to this island to start with. Cold weather affects the fertility and hatchability of the eggs. It affects the available food supply, and it can mean life or death to the helpless youngsters in their nests.

In confinement a great number of nature's hazards can be reduced. Nesting sites should be placed where extreme climatic conditions can do no harm. Shelter and light are more important together than either of these alone.

How disappointing it is to have a nest of valuable youngsters drowned in a thunderstorm through lack of a pane of glass or a piece of glass substitute in the right place, or how disappointing to have them starved by the parent birds because the nesting site provided, and adapted and improved by the parent birds, happens to be in the darkest corner of the aviary, making it well nigh impossible to see the young ones' mouths, wavering and wagging for sus-

115

tenance until exhausted.

Too much foliage, too much heather, too much gorse, too much of similar materials is harmful. An excess restricts movement, harbours mice, and makes casual observation tedious and uninteresting. It allows the timid to hide instead of getting on with their courtship or being courted. Indeed, I have a strong suspicion that a bare aviary that allows the inmates to keep on the move and get introduced as it were, is likely to lead to much greater success than one that is burdened down with heaps of this or that, enabling the birds to sulk and hide away.

I remember seeing a pair of Bramblefinches in an aviary where no provision whatsoever was made for them to nest. They did a most unusual thing for these birds, but what one must realise was the obvious. They made a nest on the ground by shaping it with their bodies, going round and round until the perfect shape was produced for the safe deposit of their eggs.

The lesson to be learnt from this episode, surely, is that if the birds are in condition they will make every effort to nest, and if their surroundings prevent them from mixing all the time this condition will not be reached.

SHORT BREEDING SEASON

The tragedy of our breeding season is its short duration. April, May and June are the months of sweet optimism, while in July we expect some results for our twelve months' anticipation. August denotes moulting time for ninety per cent of the birds, and, therefore, the end of the season, with the exception perhaps of a few later nesters such as the Bullfinch.

116

April, then, is the time when your breeding programme should have been well thought out and preparation well in hand. By that time your mind should be fully made up. It is far wiser to have a plan and to stick to it right through the season, only making changes if circumstances warrant them.

Your past experience in dealing with difficult varieties also counts for a lot. If you have been successful in breeding Bullfinches the knowledge gained from knowing their moods, habits, feeding and rearing methods puts you in a favourable position to hybridize with the hen Bullfinch. Likewise, the knowledge you have gained from rearing the Chaffinch or Bramblefinch is of great value for producing and rearing hybrids using one or the other of either sex to other British finches.

This advanced knowledge and experience applies to most of the hybrids and it is a safe argument to advance when breeding mules. Would you have the confidence to start out from scratch to produce good mules without first having had experience of pure Canary breeding? Would you have the confidence to produce Siskin mules without first having some experience with Siskins on their own and Canaries on their own? I think not.

Most readers will agree that the greatest handicap with which breeders are faced is the problem of possessing pairs of birds that are in condition together. Canaries are usually more advanced than British birds as obviously they have been domesticated over a long period and also are usually housed in warmer surroundings than our own native birds.

From a muling point of view this could lead to a round or two of clear, infertile eggs, wasting valuable time and using up irreplaceable energy. This state of affairs can be counteracted successfully by using a cock Canary with

Figure 14.2   **The Nest.**
This photograph shows a successful breeding pair — a nest of Goldfinch x Bullfinch hybrids with cock Goldfinch and hen Bullfinch doing their job properly. The chicks are forward and the parents

118

your hen, and getting a round of pure Canaries at first. If, after this, the finch you are intending to use appears to be getting into condition introduce him in time to fertilize the hen in her second round, and by judicious observation these methods should secure the most productive results in the shortest space of time.

Experience is very necessary in order to tell almost at a casual glance whether a bird is: (a) in condition; (b) nearing its prime condition; or (c) in some cases never likely to reach such condition. If one is in doubt the advice of a more experienced neighbour is well worth while.

Goldfinches and Linnets usually have obvious tell-tale marks of condition. Likewise the Chaffinch and Bramblefinch. The Goldfinch loses its black beak, the Linnet intensifies the colour of its beak, while the Chaffinch's and Bramblefinch's head, beak and back colours undergo a very marked colour intensification. These remarks apply to the cock birds.

With most hens the physical changes are not quite so obvious, but a hen bird in breeding condition acts in a lively, spirited manner, getting rid of surplus fat and looking for potential nesting sites.

The Chaffinch is the earliest of nesters in this country, their nests very often being noticed before the full completion of the new leaves. Linnets and Greenfinches come next in their breeding cycle, followed by the Siskin, Redpoll, Bramblefinch, etc.

The Bullfinch in confinement varies very considerably, depending on winter housing, food, etc. If they are late in the summer before taking any active interest in nesting do not despair as I have known successful results in late July and August.

DO NOT INTERFERE

By judicious observation a lot can be done to help the inmates of your aviary to get on with their nesting activities. By this I do not recommend perpetual interference. The less interference the better, but there is a difference between help and interference.

If you have two pairs of birds in a small enclosure for breeding purposes, and you notice that one of the cock birds is paying close attention to a certain hen then watch this aviary at odd times for several days, and see that the interest of the bird is uninterrupted because sometimes such a bird adopts very aggressive attitudes to the other pair no matter of which sex they may be.

This can apply to Canaries as some of these hardy out-of-door strains can be very pugnacious for a few weeks when no doubt a jealous possessiveness replaces their usual calm indifference to their neighbours.

Again, how often one has hen birds of all species that have made up their minds to nest. This is confirmed by carrying beakfulls of building materials and depositing them nowhere in particular, but usually showing some marked preference for a site which you, as the provider of the sites in the aviary did not intend to be used for the rearing of the family.

This site should be made, therefore, more comfortable, and by that I mean the surface of the site base should be such that immediate building operations can be performed, and, if necessary, help can be given.

FICKLE BIRDS

Hen Chaffinches are fickle in this respect, perhaps owing to the fact that they like to do quite a bit of weaving in their process of nest construction, and when weaving commences they do not always feel quite at home with the material they have available and the artificial base on which they have to work.

So it is advantageous to place a rough outline of a nest in the selected site. Many materials or articles can be used. Wood-wool or the fine grade of wood-shavings will suffice, or a cup-shaped sisal or string nest in which they can proceed. Yet another is an old or unused nest.

Anything will do, but it is important that something is done or else you will find the eggs deposited on the floor or even in the seed pan, and it would be annoying to think that some of them may have been fertile!

This nest building assistance can be given to other species if you observe that some help is required, but quick action is advised as the time between the commencement of building to laying the first egg can vary from a matter of a day or two to even a week or two, so it is wiser to play safe.

So much for these seasonal hints. The subject is large and cannot be fully covered in a few words as most species have their own peculiar fads and fancies. Even the same species has its own individual ideas, thereby making it difficult to have hard and fast rules.

I have mentioned in the appropriate chapters the materials required by all the species of birds when constructing their nests. Birds cannot make the best type of nest from dry materials, and you will find that if you scatter on the floor of your aviary in not too large a heap the necessary materials, moisture will condition and soften them to the required standard.

In cages the materials should not be allowed to get too dry or dirty as the builders of the nest will not be able to make much shape with such materials.

Sisal is the best material one can use for all birds' nests, and this is known as binder or balign twine. The second is thicker, and when cut into short lengths not more than 3 inches long, can be easily unravelled so that each piece resembles hair in its texture.

USE SHORT LENGTHS

It is most important that the length of these pieces does not exceed 3 inches as I have seen some nasty accidents with birds carrying larger pieces. They can get hooked or wound up in the most amazing ways when carrying large pieces of sisal and pushing through the bushes, twigs or perches of the aviary.

Grasses, bents, etc., already mentioned, can be pulled out of the bottom of any hedgerow, and are better when they are two or three years old. Wool, again of short lengths, is favoured and any old bits or colour attracts those who can make use of it.

Twigs should be wiry, no thicker than the lead in a pencil, and not too brittle. Cotton wool can be stuck in the wire netting or half under a stone so that the bird using it has to tug out the piece she requires. This prevents her carrying too much about. A little used often is better for construction purposes than one big lump.

Nesting sites have also been referred to, and this is a matter where individual fanciers can use their ingenuity. I have emphasized that too much cover should not be provided, but it must be suitable. Some lucky fanciers have naturally planted aviaries and these bushes, generally of an evergreen type such as box or laurel, can get very dense.

Heather and wild broom can be tied in small bunches; so can other twigs of a non-prickly nature, and in the centre of these can be placed the wicker or sisal baskets. The baskets only provide a good firm level base, cup-shaped, of course, so that the bird can build her nest right in this receptacle.

Many fanciers prefabricate nesting sites by fixing foliage and twigs on to a length of board or alternatively, tie them on to a short broom handle or stick. These units can be fixed with nails or wire into their required position under some form of cover.

The prefabricated bush can be made by tying a large bunch of twigs of such materials as heather, elm suckers, birch, privet, box, etc., either like a bunch of flowers, some-where near the middle, or on to a stake, leaving the bunch protruding at least 18 inches above the top of the stake. Into the centre of these bunches can be placed small boxes, flower pots half-filled with turf, straw, grass, etc.

Odd bits of wire netting can also be used shaped round a 4 inch flower pot, so that the necessary shape and size are arrived at.

If these bunches do not get too dirty or rotten they can be used for several seasons and it is always nicer and neater to place a few twigs of an evergreen type around the nesting sites to freshen them up and give an added attraction.

Figure 14.3 **Breeding Pair.**
Here we see one type of nest pan which may be provided for breeding birds.
(Courtesy: Cage and Aviary Birds).

15
Rearing Hybrids

Figure 15.1 **Good Feeders** — Siskins make exceptionally good feeders and would make ideal foster parents later in the season.
(Photo courtesy: M.K.V. Carr)

15
REARING HYBRIDS

I have described in detail the methods to use when rearing mules in cages. The same process hardly applies to hybrids, since if attempting to rear them in cages, we are up against problems of different sexes being in different conditions of breeding maturity.

Having two hens of different breeds with one cock bird of another breed could reduce this risk, and an example of this would be a Goldfinch cock housed with a Chaffinch hen and a Bullfinch hen. The Goldfinch can be conditioned fairly early, the Chaffinch is naturally an early nester while the Bullfinch's calendar is of a wider span. It is obvious, therefore, that plenty of accommodation is necessary and this can be provided only by the use of aviaries.

It is possible by this method to have the Goldfinch mate with the early Chaffinch, and when she has finished the hen Bullfinch could be getting ready for receiving her mate. I only quote these examples to describe my point. Other species of birds can be used in the same way.

As the personality of birds varies considerably, however, this cannot be used as a hard and fast rule. The personality of the cock bird, for instance, does not allow him to have another hen in close contact that interferes, with perhaps fatal results. Here breeders' own observations and sense have to be employed and a decision made on whether or not to remove the hen concerned.

It is not advisable to move a cock bird from his mate in hybrid breeding as he can be of great help when feeding the youngsters and very often takes over their complete care (after a period of ten days or so after hatching) while the hen starts another nest.

As the season is of short duration it is advisable to keep a diary of events, such as: (a) date of any noticeable interest taken between the sexes; (b) date of commencement of nest building; (c) date of laying first egg; (d) date of laying last egg.

With this information recorded it is safe to examine the eggs for fertility at around the fifth day of incubation. This can be done by taking them lightly between finger and thumb and holding them up to the light. The sunlight is sufficient, but if this is not strong enough to give a clear indication of whether an egg is "full" or not, a strong torch or electric bulb should be used.

A fertile egg is obvious. It is dark and the whole inside blurred. The infertile egg shows clearly the yolk sac suspended in the egg white. The darker marked eggs are more difficult to see through (e.g. Chaffinch or Bramblefinch) but by judicious handling and twisting the egg between the finger and the thumb, a position will be arrived at that sets the whole scene in perfect relief.

REMOVE INFERTILE EGGS

If it is found that all the eggs are infertile, remove them immediately, destroy the nest and see that there is plenty of building material available for the construction of another nest. The material of the destroyed nest can be used again, of course, if it is sweet and clean.

If the eggs are fertile and you can rely on the parent birds to properly feed the youngsters, leave them alone and introduce the rearing foods that you intend to use. If the eggs are plentiful and only a few are fertile remove the infertile ones so that the good eggs have all the available heat of the hen for incubation.

If only one egg is fertile leave one or two other eggs in the nest right through the time the bird is sitting as those eggs act as companions and give the youngsters some support in the nest, both for their bodies and their feet. Their toes and claws need some exercise, and in a flat bottomed nest on their own young birds are not too happy. Faulty toes and claws can be attributed to the lack of support in the nest.

The age at which the young birds leave their nests varies according to how well they have been fed, both from the point of view of the quantity and quality. If the food contains the wrong proteins and carbohydrates and is unbalanced, young birds do not thrive as quickly as they do when fed on a properly balanced diet. This is dealt with in the chapter on feeding, as rearing itself is a matter of physical help and control.

GOOD FEEDERS

Parent birds when feeding their young, are very varied in their approach to this problem. Birds that have proved themselves to be quite capable of doing the job properly usually keep this high standard, and when their past likes and dislikes are known one can supply their likes and cease worrying over their future behaviour.

Those that have not been proved want watching carefully until you are satisfied they are going on the right lines.

Those that are hopeless and do not appear to bother about feeding are the ones that cause the work and the headaches. If they are lazy feeders, that is, feed occasionally, brood the youngsters far too much, and the youngsters always appear to be hungry, then hand rearing methods should be adopted until the young ones are grown and more satisfied with life.

Once such hopeless feeders are known they should not be relied on at all, and foster parents, if available, should be brought into use. Greenfinches are useful in this respect as their breeding period extends through the spring and summer. Siskins are exceptionally good feeders, but are later nesters and are not available until later in the summer.

Another point to remember is that sometimes a hen suddenly forsakes her nest for no apparent reason, and if any of her eggs are fertile and are likely to be lost because of the lack of a foster parent, one's disappointment can be very great. Border and Roller Canaries, Glosters, Lizards and Red Factors — all these varieties of Canaries are usually good feeders and should be used in an emergency.

Nor should anyone fight shy of using any species of British bird as a foster parent. We should copy the Cuckoo sometimes and deposit eggs into another nest, either in an emergency or if one has good reason to suspect that the motherly instincts of the natural parent are at fault.

CHOICE OF FOSTER PARENT

It is important, however, that the right foster parent for the right breed of youngster should be used for feeding, although not necessarily incubating. There are many finches that rear entirely on live food for the first week at least. It is not much good, therefore, putting such a "meat eater" in the care of a "vegetarian". As an example, any offspring of a Chaffinch x Bramblefinch pairing ("meat eater") would not thrive for long under the wing of a Canary ("vegetarian") but a young Canary would be reared perfectly under a Chaffinch or Bramblefinch hen.

The Greenfinch hen can be considered in the main to be a "vegetarian", Bullfinch and Linnet likewise, but the Siskin, Twite, Bramblefinch, etc., are "meat eaters", "insectivorous" or "softbilled" when rearing.

The lazy feeders previously referred to seem to lack the energy to get on with the job quickly during the first two or three days after hatching. A chick does not require much, if any, food for the first twenty-four hours after hatching, having been properly nourished in the egg. Two, three or four days later however, their future lies in the balance, and any food that can be provided by the owner to stimulate the parents or the youngsters should be attended to at this stage.

One way of stimulation is to deposit attractive bits of food on the edge of the nest. This is best provided in the form of ants' eggs, cut up mealworms, soft crumbly egg food, etc. As hen finches are very clean nesters they will remove this deposited material by swallowing it, as indeed they do all the youngsters' excreta for the first few days.

Forcing them, as it were, to swallow this food in the general work of keeping things tidy and sanitary, gives them the taste and forms an introduction to anything you are hoping they will ultimately take in the more conventional manner. Small ants' eggs, egg food, etc., can also be popped into the youngsters' mouths by the owner if he wants to assist the hen and make sure they are getting enough food.

16
Feeding and Foods

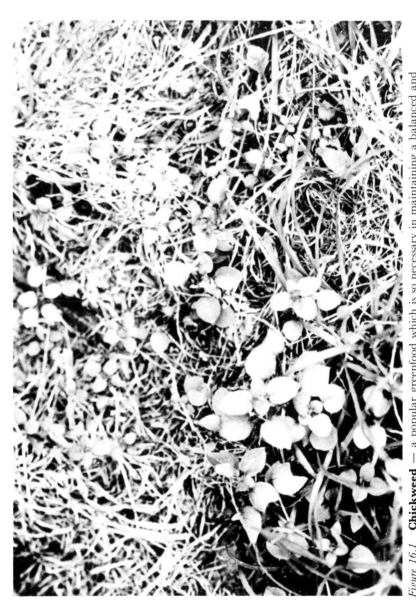

Figure 16.1 **Chickweed** — a popular greenfood which is so necessary in maintaining a balanced and varied diet.
(Courtesy: E. Howson, The Yorkshire Canary)

16

FEEDING AND FOODS

I have mentioned in the appropriate places the stock seed of all our hybridizing finches. This has been given in the simplest form as I am not a believer in giving a bit of this, a bit of that, a pinch of this or a pinch of that to birds as a titbit or even as a means of supplying them with food.'

The analysis of the foods briefly mentioned in previous chapters shows that they supply all the birds' chemical requirements and "fiddling" about with a lot of other fads and fancies, because that is all I consider them to be, adds to the work and makes the job of the hobby appear to be a lot more difficult and troublesome than is actually so.

It is necessary at the outset to say something about the nature and function of some of the most important of the food constituents and I am indebted to Dr. T. G. Taylor, M.A., Ph.D., of Reading University, for this information, as it is necessary these days to give a scientific explanation of the chemical composition of most foods.

Dr. Taylor's information and advice, given below, appeared in one of the *British Bird Breeders' Association Year Books* and I appreciate their ready permission to allow me to use this excellent summary of the various foods and their use for our birds.

Carbohydrates
The most important carbohydrates in nutrition are starch

and the various sugars, and the outer coats of seeds consist largely of another carbohydrate, cellulose. Whereas starch and sugars are very digestible, cellulose is very indigestible to most birds.

The well-known sugar glucose is present in the blood and it is derived largely from the carbohydrates of the food. All the cells of the body use the blood sugar as a source of energy and give off heat for the maintenance of body temperature as a by-product of energy utilisation. The energy for flying, and indeed for all bodily movements, comes ultimately from the blood glucose.

Fats and Oils

Fats are used also to provide heat and energy and the main reserves of energy-giving substances are in the form of fat. The fat reserves of the body come both from the fat of the food and from the excess carbohydrates eaten.

Proteins

All natural foods contain protein but the amount varies very much. The living protoplasm of all cells consists very largely of protein, which means that all tissues — muscles, liver, kidneys, etc. — are rich in this material. Skin, feathers, beaks and claws consist largely of protein and eggs contain large amounts.

Proteins are very complex substances but they are built up of relatively simple units, the amino-acids. There are about twenty distinct amino-acids and different proteins contain them in different amounts.

Some food proteins are deficient in certain amino-acids, and in order to make sure that all are present in adequate amounts it is a very good principle to feed as varied a diet as possible, so that many different proteins are fed, thus minimizing the danger of any one amino-acid being deficient.

Whenever possible it is desirable to include some food of animal origin in the diet, food such as insects, milk or egg, as animal proteins are of higher nutritional value than plant proteins because they more nearly resemble in amino-acid make-up the tissues of the bird they are to nourish.

Since eggs, baby chicks and feathers contain large amounts of protein it is particularly important that the food should contain adequate quantities of protein during the breeding and moulting season.

Vitamins

Vitamins are organic substances present in minute amounts in natural foods, which are essential for health and which result in various diseases and abnormal conditions when present in inadequate amounts. Slight deficiencies result in lack of condition.

If we could house and feed our birds as in nature, vitamin deficiencies would not occur, and it is only because we have to rely largely on dry seeds for our birds and to keep them indoors that we have to face the possibility of vitamin deficiency occurring.

The individual vitamins and practical methods of administering them are considered later in these notes.

Minerals

Minerals are present in all plant and animal cells and they are therefore essential to life. There are at least a dozen different minerals required by birds and only the most important are considered here.

Calcium (lime) is concentrated in the bones where it

occurs in combination with phosphorus. A deficiency of calcium, therefore, results in weak and poorly calcified bones, a condition known as rickets when it occurs in young birds. Calcium is also required in large amounts for egg-shell formation, as shells consist almost entirely of calcium carbonate (chalk).

Vitamin D is essential for calcium utilization and a deficiency of either Vitamin D or calcium results in poorly calcified shells or soft-shelled eggs and egg-binding is likely to occur. All seeds are very deficient in calcium.

Phosphorus is present in all soft tissues as well as in bones, and egg yolk contains large quantities. Seeds, oil seeds in particular, are fair sources of phosphorus.

Common salt or sodium chloride is a very important mineral and one which is deficient in all the usual seeds and in greenfood. It is the chief mineral present in the blood.

Many minerals such as manganese, iron, copper, cobalt and iodine are required in traces and while a deficiency of any one is not likely to occur it is a wise insurance to see that a complete mineral mixture (containing all the trace elements as well as the major mineral elements) is always available to your birds.

The seeds commonly fed to British birds can be divided into two main categories, the cereals such as canary seed, wheat and oats, and the oil seeds such as hemp, rape, linseed, niger, maw and sunflower. Buckwheat, though not a cereal, is similar in composition to them.

Cereals and oil seeds differ greatly from one another. Cereals are high in starch and relatively low in oil and protein, while oil seeds are rich in oil and protein and low in starch. Within the two categories there are, of course, differences between the different seeds and it should be appreciated that there are variations between different

138

samples of the same seed.

The following table gives the average composition of the kernels of some of the most important seeds fed to British birds.

Average percentage composition of the kernels of seeds calculated for a moisture content of 8% and a fibre content of 2%.

		Protein	Fats and Oils	Carbo- hydrates (Starch etc.)
CEREALS	Millet	12	4	68
	Wheat	13	3	73
	Groats	16	6	65
	Canary Seed	19	6	61
	Buckwheat	14	3	67
OIL-SEEDS	Hemp	21	38	25
	Maw	22	35	25
	Linseed	25	38	24
	Niger	26	43	15
	Rape	20	46	19
	Sunflower	19	43	20
WILD-SEEDS	Ryegrass	11	2	71
	Yorkshire Fog	17	18	47
	Plantain	19	9	45

The feeding of British finches during the non-breeding season presents no serious difficulties, and I would suggest a staple seed mixture of three parts cereal to one part oil seed, the varieties in each case depending on the species. It is a good idea to feed the soft food you intend to use during the breeding season once or twice a week so that they are well accustomed to it.

During the breeding season food requirements are more exacting and it is most important for the diet to be complete in every nutrient, particularly in vitamins and minerals, if success is to be achieved. A deficiency of any

139

vitamin or mineral in the diet of the hen is very liable to result in the eggs failing to hatch or in the production of weakly chicks.

Nutritional deficiencies are thought to be responsible for a very large proportion of the dead-in-shell trouble experienced by breeders.

ESSENTIAL NUTRIENTS

If an egg is to hatch, it must contain within it all the nutrients required by the developing chick, for once an egg is laid there is no way in which it can obtain them. If even one vitamin is present in insufficient amounts the embryo will continue to develop until all the vitamin is used up and then it will die.

The exact stage of incubation at which death occurs will, of course, depend on the seriousness of the deficiency and if the deficiency is very slight the chick may even develop to the stage at which the shell is chipped, only to die in its efforts to escape from the shell.

Fortunately there are only four vitamins which are likely to be deficient in the staple seed diet of British finches, namely, A, D, B_2 and B_{12}. Vitamins A and B_2 are best supplied in the form of greenfood, in which both are abundant. Vitamin D is the vitamin which is intimately concerned in the calcification of bones and egg shells.

Very few natural foods contain significant amounts of it, but, under the influence of sunlight, it is formed on the feathers from a precursor present in the oil secreted by the preen gland, and when the birds preen themselves some of the Vitamin D is taken into the beak.

There may also be direct absorption through the skin.

Figure 16.2 **Healthy Bird.**
All the essential nutrients must be available to your birds if they are to retain good health. Here we see a Canary x Bullfinch in prime condition. (*Courtesy: Cage and Aviary Birds*)

141

Birds kept in outside aviaries should not, therefore, require a dietary supply of this vitamin, but those breeding in cages indoors should be given it.

Both Vitamin D and Vitamin B_{12} may conviently be provided in the soft food used for the rearing of the young birds and which is offered at fairly frequent intervals during the winter and early spring.

There are many proprietary brands of high protein rearing foods on the market which are very suitable for feeding to British birds, but for those who would like to mix their own I give below a suitable formula. If, however, you have a formula of your own which the birds like and which is successful, stick to it!

$3\frac{1}{2}$lbs fine biscuit meal or sausage rusk
8 oz dried milk (preferably full-cream)
8 oz wheat germ
8 oz white fish meal
4 oz dried yeast
2 oz arachis oil fortified with Vitamins A and D*
*$\frac{1}{2}$ oz Adexolin mixed with 5 oz arachis oil

The above mixture is mixed to a crumbly consistency with water before feeding.

It is very difficult for the breeder to make his own mixture for the provision of the trace minerals as many of them are required in very small quantities and is better to give the birds one of the complete mineral mixtures which have been scientifically compounded and are advertised in *Cage Birds*.

Sea sand should always be available and so should fine oyster shell to provide the calcium (lime) required for bones and egg shells. Sand, oyster shell and mineral mixture may all be fed together in one vessel.

Before considering the feeding of breeding birds with young in the nest I should like to remind readers of the

142

nature of the food which a chick receives before it hatches, namely, the white and yolk of egg. Apart from water and small amounts of minerals and vitamins, egg white consists almost entirely of protein, and egg yolk of a mixture of fat and protein.

In the case of the chick of the domestic fowl all of the white and about 60% of the yolk is transformed into chick tissue during incubation. The remaining 40% of the yolk is absorbed into the body of the chick the day before hatching, and while a large part of this yolk is digested during the first two days of life it does not get completely used up for about a week.

The rate of the absorption of the yolk sac in other birds has not been studied, but it is fairly safe to assume that for the first few days after hatching the young of all birds derive a substantial amount of nourishment from the egg yolk they absorb before emerging from the shell. Nature, therefore, has given us a clue as to the sort of food which newly hatched birds need — a high protein material similar to egg yolk.

VALUE OF LIVE FOOD

Wild finches supply their young with this high protein, high fat diet in the form of insects, and the value of live ant cocoons, greenfly, etc., in rearing finches in confinement has long been recognised.

Mealworms and gentles are frequently offered in addition to or instead of "wild" insects. On a dry matter basis meal worms in a fairly advanced state of maturity contain about 50% protein and 36% fat, and gentles are somewhat similar.

There can be little doubt that live insects form the ideal food for most British finches when rearing young, but few breeders can hope to provide for their young birds to be reared exclusively on live food and it is important to have available a food which the birds will eat readily and which will, as far as possible, take the place of live food. A suitable formula for such a food has been suggested earlier in this chapter.

Live food becomes somewhat less vital as the chicks grow older, as their requirements for protein and fat decrease somewhat with age, so newly hatched chicks should have priority for any live food which is available. If live food is completely unobtainable it may be replaced by finely chopped hard boiled egg mixed with the soft food (two parts soft food, one part egg) for the first few days, gradually decreasing the proportion of egg as the chicks grow older.

GREEN FOOD IS IMPORTANT

Although insects form a large proportion of the total food intake of nestling finches, the unripe seed of wild, crop and garden plants is also fed in quantity. Green food is, therefore, regarded as being virtually essential for British Hardbills when rearing young. Chickweed, shepherds' purse, dandelion and plantain are among the most common of the weeds which provide valuable seeds during the breeding season.

The seeding heads of such grasses as rye grass, cocksfoot and timothy also provide useful food, and I can imagine that breeders of British birds must be tempted to allow some of their broccoli plants to go to seed to provide

144

rearing food for their birds.

Just as good soft food may be looked upon as a substitute for live food, soaked seeds can make up a shortage of fresh wild seeds. If the seeds are allowed to soak for several days so that they start to germinate chemical changes occur in them as a result of which they come to resemble the immature seeds normally eaten by wild birds. Great care must of course be taken to wash the soaked seeds thoroughly and to remove all uneaten seeds daily. Sour or mouldy seeds are fatal to young birds.

While I regard germinating seeds as nutritionally superior to soaked seeds, the practical difficulties attending the maintenance of a continuous supply of germinating seeds are considerable and overnight soaking is probably the most satisfactory procedure for most breeders.

The suggestions I have made for feeding British finches during the breeding season are, I think, in keeping with the feeding methods employed by practical breeders — live food, a protein rich soft food, green food and soaked seeds. They are also in keeping, as far as possible, with nature's methods. Hard, dry seeds which, in captivity, are fed to finches during the non-breeding season are only available in the wild state for a very limited period of the year — at harvest time.

USE OF HARD SEEDS

Before this time the wild seeds are soft and immature, and soon after harvest time when the seeds are shed, the autumn rains soak them on the ground. For this reason it would seem to be a good principle to continue feeding soft food and soaked seed to young birds long after they have

145

left the nest and to introduce hard seeds into the diet very slowly and carefully. This is certainly nature's way. Hard seeds are not available to young finches in the wild, until they are several months old.

Throughout these notes I have constantly stressed the value of natural foods and the importance of following natural principles as far as possible. When discussing proteins I mentioned the importance of feeding as varied a diet as possible in order to insure against a deficiency of any particular amino-acid and a varied diet, such as wild birds enjoy, is far less likely to be deficient in vitamins and minerals also than a more restricted diet.

Remember that a diet of hard seed is at best only a substitute for the fresh seeds and insects enjoyed by birds in the wild state, and the more you are able to supply the foods eaten under natural conditions the greater the chances of successful breeding. A well balanced soft food and soaked seed can, however, be of extreme value when live food and fresh green food are scarce.

There is nothing that can with advantage be added to the foregoing notes by Dr. Taylor. Little research has been done into the nutritional requirements of birds kept in cages and aviaries. Dr. Taylor is a scientist who is also a breeder of birds, and we are indeed lucky to have the benefit of his research and advice.

17
Exhibiting

Figure 17.1 **At the Show.**
(Courtesy: E. Howson, *The Yorkshire Canary)*

17

EXHIBITING

The exhibition world is certainly the place where the values of mules and hybrids are correctly assessed. Any rare production of either of these crosses is quickly appraised by the large number of enthusiasts throughout the British Isles, and it is only at the open or local shows that one has the chance of meeting more of these fanciers and their own products.

A great deal of optimistic expectancy ripples over the inquisitive surface of enthusiasts during the breeding season, wondering what the forthcoming show season will produce in the way of exhibits. Many rumours, of course, spread before this pleasant social season is with us, so some ideas are firmly fixed before the "rumour" is finally seen, and it is then that the merits and faults are pronounced.

It is important, therefore, that new or very rare crosses that have been achieved during the breeding season should be introduced to the public in some form or another, and the witnesses of these rarities should be carefully selected. The first showing is then made easier, and interest in the bird is more readily appreciated by experts and novices alike.

I have seen rarities shown for the first time that have not been accepted. I have seen others greatly appraised that the breeders did not realise were of real value and interest until they were exhibited, and it is only by contact at exhibitions that the real assessment of the value or rarity can be gauged.

The Light mule is always of value as it is a rare occurence. The value, therefore, of any parent stock that is capable of this reproduction is immense, working on the assumption that other youngsters can be produced in the following years.

The parent birds that can produce large, yellow, good coloured mules of any variety are also of value, as the good mule is an exception rather than the rule and the best is always sought after.

When it comes to the hybrids that are bred from known species, most enthusiasts have the perfect bird in their mind's eye, and unflighted birds that appear every year are valued with past successes as the yardstick of judgement, and here the novice lacking such experience should seek the opinion of more knowledgeable fanciers.

Large shows always cater for the mule and hybrid section to the best of their financial ability, as many classes as are economically possible being provided. Smaller shows, with local knowledge of available exhibits and the realisation that they will be drawing exhibits from a limited area tend to be cautious and put on the minimum of classification. This minimum consists of (a) class for Canary mules; (b) class for hybrids between two British birds. An improvement on this is (a) and (b) above with the addition of (c) unflighted mules and (d) unflighted hybrids, (a) and (b) being restricted to flighted or old birds.

Another class provided by many is (e) miniature mules. In this case the prize goes to the smallest bird, of course, showing the best characteristic colour, markings, staging, etc. This class was introduced to cater for the man who bred mules using the smallest type of Canary as opposed to the larger varieties, and some interesting birds have been exhibited in such classes. If this miniature class were not provided such small varieties of mules would have to compete with the larger type bred from Norwich, Yorkshire or Border Canaries and on size alone would not get a look in.

It is worth recording that some of these miniature mules bred from Red Factor Canaries are delightful from the colour point of view and most interesting to see. In these cases the miniature mule class attracts the exhibits that normally remain at home, benefiting the show and the visiting public.

Another variation in the provision of classes is to separate Bullfinch hybrids from other breeds. Most readers will agree it is difficult to compare with fairness in the same class all hybrids, since the Bullfinch hybrid always gains so much from the colour and character of both parents.

As in hybrids so in mules. The competition between, say, the large Greenfinch mules and the naturally smaller Siskin mule is not fair to the exhibitor or the judge, as little birds could be the perfection of their respective breeds but when in competition together one has to take second place.

Any readers interested in the presentaion of mules and hybrids at public shows and with any influence on the proper provision of economic classification should see to it that birds of similar type are in competition one with another, rather than all lumped together in an "Any Variety Mule" class. Goldfinch mules should be catered for separately. Linnet and Twite mules can go together.

Siskin and Redpoll mules can also compete together from their size point of view. The Greenfinch mule could come in the "Any Other Variety" class and have no other competitor unless, of course, a rarer mule makes its appearance and then it can be exhibited in this class.

The existence of the Light, Clear or Variegated mules makes it imperative for a separate class to be provided.

At the well supported national shows a further breakdown of types occurs in the classification inasmuch as Clear classes are provided, Lightly Variegated, Heavily Variegated, Yellow or Jonque Goldfinch mules, Buff Goldfinch mules, and so on, right through the commoner varieties, which one must agree is the perfect classification. I am sure no show promoters resent any elaboration on the provision of many classes, providing full support is forthcoming, and in this commercial world anything that is likely to show a profit is well looked after.

This classification can be further extended by stipulating an old or flighted bird and a young or unflighted bird. Also the whole lot can be duplicated by the division of these classes into **Champion** or **Novice** status exhibitors. It is obvious, therefore, that the limit to the perfect all-embracing provision of all these classes is very considerable.

The same position arises in the hybrid classes. Bullfinch hybrids should be separated from other types and also old and young birds should be catered for separately. Of course, good young birds can beat mediocre old birds, but the young mediocre birds cannot beat the older birds. However, perhaps after another year it would not necessarily be in the mediocre category as all British birds, mules and hybrids improve enormously with time, up to a certain age, when a deterioration becomes apparent. This deterioration is more pronounced in Bullfinch hybrids as they appear to age quicker than many other types, and after five years one can say in the main that they are past their peak of perfection.

152

Again, in the largest shows Bullfinch hybrids are broken down into Goldfinch x Bullfinch; Greenfinch x Bullfinch; Canary x Bullfinch; A.O.V. Bullfinch hybrid, all flighted or old birds. The unflighted or young birds can be separately classed or lumped together in "Any Variety Bullfinch Hybrid" class.

The more common varieties of hybrid are not necessarily more plentiful, strange though it may seem, and I cannot understand or explain why this is so. Perhaps as most Bullfinch hybrids secure the supreme honours, breeders of the other varieties feel they are not worth showing in such competition. Nevertheless, for all that, show promoting societies have a duty to provide as many other classes as possible so that unusual birds get in the public eye, and what hybrid is not unusual after all?

All Greenfinch hybrids, Chaffinch hybrids, Linnet hybrids and so on, come in here and the larger the number bred the more the likelihood of an extended classification.

It is almost a repetition of the old expression, "Which comes first, the chicken or the egg?". Do societies have to provide the classification to tempt breeders to support the classes, or do breeders persuade show societies they have the birds, but only a limited classification is provided?

I have dealt with this question of classification at length as it will help to explain the situation that exists at the present time. If any fancier reads this book hoping to get an understanding of the subject before planning his breeding programme, he should not be deterred by the position he sees at the moment. He should proceed as his interests dictate and thereafter the breeding results obtained by fanciers will help them to secure the classification they want at shows.

The **National British Bird and Mule Club** is the

Figure 17.2 **Exhibiting.**
All birds should be shown in a clean condition and in a neat and clean cage. This Canary x Bullfinch hybrid shows clearly the striated markings on the back which distinguish it from a Greenfinch x Bullfinch. These distinct markings are important in gaining show points.
(*Courtesy: Cage and Aviary Birds, photo courtesy:* E.V. Breeze Jones)

154

specialist society that most enthusiasts consider worth while joining as medals and prizes are given to successful breeders and exhibitors. This society also sets standards of perfection for all our native finches, mules and hybrids, which are accepted as the ultimate goal of perfection. Colour and sizes of cages are also recommended for guidance so that newcomers to the hobby will know precisely where they stand, thereby saving considerable expense on equipment that is not generally accepted.

The following tables set out the points system of arriving at the perfect specimen of Light and Dark Canary mules or hybrids, for exhibition purposes and if studied will convey the situation briefly and clearly.

These standards may be applied as laid down, or they may be varied somewhat in regard to the number of points allotted to the various prominent features detailed. When a person is judging Light Canary hybrids, special attention must be paid to the approach to the two standards of perfection, viz., the clear and the evenly marked birds.

In a Ticked or Variegated class those birds having size, shape and good quality, and possessing plumage approximately nearest the Clear or the Evenly-Marked standards, are undoubtedly of the highest value as show birds. Those birds not having any standard character about the variegation are of much less value as show specimens.

155

CLEAR, TICKED AND LIGHTLY VARIEGATED
CANARY HYBRIDS

Size.   To be of good size, compatible with that of the parents   10

Shape.   To be of stout, cone shape, with broad, bold head, and close-fitting wings and tail   10

Markings.   To be distinctly characteristic of both parents and the clearer the plumage the better   20

Colour.   To be deep and rich in colour naturally, and when colour-fed, to be considerably intensified   10

Quality.   The plumage to exhibit the highest possible smooth, glossy surface throughout   20

Condition.   To be sound in condition in every part   15

Steadiness.   The bolder and firmer the stand on the perch, the better   10

Staging.   To be shown in clean condition and in a neat and clean cage   5

Maximum points 100

NEGATIVE PROPERTIES. — Wildness, crouching, puffiness, broken or missing feathers, deformities of body, wings, legs or feet, poor quality of markings, bad conditions, etc.

EVENLY MARKED CANARY HYBRIDS

Size.   To be of good size, compatible with that of the parents   10

Shape.   To be of stout, cone shape with broad, bold head, and close-fitting wings and tail   10

Markings.   Whether eyes, wing or tail, any or all to be as even on both sides of the bird as possible and not to run beyond the technical regions of markings proper   35

Colour.   To be rich and deep in tone naturally, and, when colour-fed to be very highly intensified   10

Quality.   The feathers to be perfect, with a satin-like surface   10

Condition.   To be of the very best in every respect   10

Steadiness.   The bolder and firmer the position on the perch, the better   10

Staging. To be shown in a clean condition and in a neat and clean cage   5

Maximum points 100

NEGATIVE PROPERTIES — Badly balanced markings; markings running beyond their proper regions, or being so faint and indistinct that they barely outline the character of a mark; crouching, indifferent shape; poor feather; deformity in any part; wildness; undersize — all these failings reduce points when present.

156

DARK CANARY HYBRIDS

(This standard also applies to hybrids between two British birds.)

Size. The larger the better, compatible with that of the parents	10
Shape. To be of stout, cone shape with broad, bold head, and close-fitting wings and tail	10
Markings. To show distinctly, and nicely blended, the chief characteristics, markings, and colours of both parents	20
Colour To be rich, deep and distinct, and when colour-fed, to be greatly intensified	10
Quality. The plumage to possess the highest possible smooth, glossy surface throughout	20
Condition. To be sound in condition in every part	10
Steadiness. To be bold, firm, steady and fearless on the perch	15
Staging. To be shown in a clean condition and in a neat and clean cage	5

Maximum points 100

NEGATIVE PROPERTIES — Wildness, crouching, poor shape, poor or broken feathers, missing claws, indistinct colours and markings, undersize, lameness or deformity — all these detract from the points of a show specimen.

BRITISH BIRD HYBRIDS

Size.	15
Shape. Stout cone shape	10
Markings and Colour. To show distinctly and nicely blended the chief characteristics of both parents	30
Quality of Feather and Condition	25
Steadiness and Staging	20

Maximum points 100

Bullfinch hybrids stand very high in this class

To complete this chapter on exhibiting, I set out below the sizes and shape of the correct cages, with acknowledgements to the N.B.B. & M.C.

BRITISH HARDBILLS, MULES AND HYBRIDS

Size No. 2. For Goldfinch, Lesser Redpoll, Siskin, Linnet, Twite and Mealy Redpoll; Redpoll and Siskin mules, and other British bird hybrids whose size does not exceed the

Hardbills in this category, including Redpoll x Bullfinch.

Length 11 inches, height $9\frac{1}{2}$ inches, width $4\frac{1}{2}$ inches. The wires are No. 14 gauge and $\frac{5}{8}$ inches apart, centre to centre. The drinking hole is 1 inch in diameter. The bottom and top rails remain the same.

Size No. 3 For Bullfinch, Greenfinch, Chaffinch, Brambling, Yellow, Reed and Cirl Buntings; Bullfinch hybrids, Goldfinch, Linnet, Twite and Greenfinch mules, and other British bird hybrids whose size is similar to the Hardbills in this category.

Length 12 inches, height 10 inches, width 5 inches. The wires are No. 14 gauge and $\frac{3}{4}$ inch apart, centre to centre. The drinking hole is $1\frac{1}{8}$ inches diameter. The bottom and top rails are again the same.

Size No. 4 For Hawfinch, Crossbill, Corn Bunting, Snow Bunting and Lapland Bunting.

Length 14 inches, height 12 inches, width $6\frac{1}{2}$ inches. The wires are No. 14 gauge and 1 inch apart, centre to centre. The drinking hole is $1\frac{1}{4}$ inches in diameter. In this case the bottom rail is 2 inches high and the top rail $1\frac{1}{2}$ inches at the outsides, sloping to $\frac{3}{4}$ inch in the centre.

The decorative treatment recommended is black outside (top, bottom, back and sides) with the inside and front (wires and both rails) Aspinall's Jade Green. (Cage No. 1 has been discontinued.)

BRITISH SOFTBILLS

Softbills should always be shown in as large a cage as possible, being so much more active than Hardbills. The following sizes are suggested:

Size No. 5. Small Softbills up to the size of a Waxwing. 16

inches long x 13 inches high x 8 inches wide.

Size No. 6   Thrush family. 18 inches long x 15 inches high x 12 inches wide.

Size No. 7   All other large Softbills. 24 inches long x 20 inches high x 14 inches wide.

Food and water vessels inside cage. White interior and black wire fronts.

Figure 17.3 **Position** — a bird's position on the perch when showing should be as bold and firm as possible. This Bramblefinch x Chaffinch hybrid exhibits a good alert stance and expression.

(Photo courtesy: M.K.V. Carr)

18
Conclusions

Figure 18.1 **Objectives** — the breeding of mules and hybrids provides an absorbing hobby and pursuit for many. The rewards may be few but when a good mule, such as this Siskin Mule, is produced it all becomes worthwhile.

18

CONCLUSIONS

In this book so far I have endeavoured to give all the varieties of hybrids that have been bred, or are likely to be produced with birds with which one can attempt to breed. I have mentioned aviaries, building materials for nests and also sites for these nests. I have discussed the feeding of young and old stock, fertility of eggs, the exhibition world and proceeded right through the whole season's work that bird lovers enjoy, starting in the spring and culminating in the social life enjoyed at the winter shows.

In doing all this I have avoided any reference to the disappointments that are bound to occur, for as we all know life consists of rather more disappointments, troubles and sorrow than it does of successes, luck and joy. But fortunately our minds do not register for long the unsavoury side of life; the happiest moments always stand out bright and clear and are not dimmed to any large extent by time.

However, I should be failing in my efforts to put mule and hybrid breeding in their right perspective if I did not say quite definitely that your failures and disappointments are likely to be much greater than your successes over a long period. The expression "beginner's luck" is often heard and it is amazing that this beginner's luck actually exists for one or two seasons, but eventually the law of averages will play its part. There is no doubt that because

163

of this, the interest in this breeding "agin Nature" has its hold on the enthusiast, and when one views a season's results any successful rearing is prized quite highly. It is only right, therefore, that the prize should be valued accordingly.

To begin with, the climate takes its toll in casualties, and can retard a bird's reproductive desires. If proper safeguards are not taken it can also eliminate all that one has achieved. For instance, I have heard of aviaries being blown away. Was this due to lack of a suitable safeguard? I have heard of aviary roofs damaged by snow, thereby releasing all the inmates. Again was there any safeguard against that?

I have heard of youngsters being drowned in their nests, rats and mice crawling in the aviaries, the former killing most if not all the inmates, and the latter frightening incubating hens off their nest so that the eggs are starved before morning, killing the soon-to-be-hatched chick.

This vision of a bird-lover's "chamber of horrors" can be eliminated if sufficient forethought is given to the management, design and the practice of birdkeeping and breeding. You might argue, however, that these risks could apply only to outdoor aviaries where vermin prowl unmolested, where in fact the climate is uncontrolled, where hawks, owls, grey squirrels, cats, dogs, rats, mice, voles, foxes, badgers — the lot — have free access and know no boundaries.

But how many fanciers, I wonder, have heard of mice and rats breaking into what one has always thought to be a vermin-proof structure? How many cats have entered a door not properly closed? How many grey squirrels have scampered along a row of breeding cages? Dogs, children . . . the list could be almost as long as the animals that went into Noah's Ark!

Forgive me if this picture I paint appears distorted, but believe me it must be depicted so that one is not lulled into a false sense of security, for sooner or later something will happen and the old saying "Forewarned is forearmed" still rings true.

I have mentioned elsewhere the danger of using nest building materials that are longer than $2\frac{1}{2}$ inches to 3 inches in length, as I have seen nasty accidents arise when the nesting birds get hung up in branches and twigs, sometimes by their necks, sometimes by their feet. And talking of feet, I have also seen some nasty accidents arise through close-fittings rings hooking on to sharp twigs, thorns and even damaged wire netting, especially the rough edges left when cutting has taken place, with the bird hanging or even breaking its leg.

Older and experienced fanciers will appreciate these sentiments. Younger ones, particularly those starting from scratch, will know nothing of these pitfalls and I hope these paragraphs will help them to avoid what costly experience has taught the older ones.

Disease, man's enemy in every form of life on this earth, whether it be in animals, birds or plants, occupy many minds in more ways than one, and I am disappointed that so little research has been carried out on this subject where cage birds are concerned. The poultry industry, which I consider is the one most closely allied to the cage bird fancy, has devoted tens of thousands of pounds to this research at various centres. Commercial firms selling foods with the correct drug to counteract certain diseases have played their part, as have also manufacturing chemists in order to stimulate the sales of a medicine.

All these organizations are doing their best to find out

165

how drugs and medicines can help to fight disease, and as the poultry business is a very vast business with a colossal annual turnover, such research is bound to go forward. It is hoped that a lot of the information obtained will be of benefit to bird lovers whose birds are facing germs similar to those affecting poultry.

Some of these poultry diseases are known, of course, in birds. Coccidiosis, enteritis, typhoid, asthma, and aspergillosis are just a few, and drugs in both liquid and granular form have been discovered for administering to affected birds. Antibiotics are now almost a household word, but the extent of their curing abilities and the amount to be administered to the domestic pet bird has in most instances yet to be determined. Let us hope that interested research chemists will soon devote some of their efforts for the benefit of birdkeepers.

The proprietary remedies available for the control of parasites such as lice, fleas, mites, are of course eminently useful for treating birds, and here again, this field has been the subject of modern research with vast improvements on the preventives of bygone days.

May I conclude by expressing the hope that this book will be of some help to those who have been prompted to read it, because obviously the subject matter is one of their interests in life. I have found it interesting to write, and offer my sincere thanks to those who have helped me to compile it. I hope that when the time comes for a new edition, some of the crosses named in the previous chapters as probabilities will have become living entities, and that man's knowledge of genetics and the cure or avoidance of diseases and other matters will go forward to greater heights.

19

Cagebirds
and the Law

Figure 19.1 **Protected** — both these birds are protected by law and may not be sold alive unless close ringed and bred in captivity.

Top: Blackbird
Bottom: Ring Ouzel

19

CAGE BIRDS AND THE LAW

Wild birds are protected by the law, the main act concerned with this being *The Protection of Birds Act, 1954*. Bird fanciers should make themselves aware of the current legislation because, generally speaking, ignorance is no excuse if an offence is committed. We are grateful to the **Royal Society for the Protection of Birds** for supplying information on this quite complex subject.

In a concise form, the position at the time of going to press is as follows:

1. *The Protection of Birds Act, 1954*, Section 1 gives protection to all wild birds and prohibits trapping and possession of a recently taken individual. Certain exceptions are made in the case of a species considered harmful to man's interests, e.g. bullfinch, but the protection of birds under Section 6 (see below) will still apply with regard to sale.

2. Section 6, 1(a), of the same Act prohibits the sale or exchange or possession or advertising for any bird included in the **Fourth Schedule** (see below) to the Act. This Schedule includes all of the species associated with aviculture plus the birds of prey. The exceptions to this prohibition are those birds which have been both bred in captivity and are close-ringed. You will note that both these provisions must apply and that it is not enough that the bird has been bred in captivity but not ringed or, alternatively, ringed with a close-ring whilst in the wild nest. The Act does not clarify what is meant by a close-ring but this has been dealt with in case law. It has been taken to mean a continuous metal band incapable of being taken apart without damage. The Courts also accept that it is the size for the particular species as decided by the ring manufacturers in conjunction with the specialist societies. In

169

practical terms, it invariably means resorting to a test as to whether the ring can or cannot be removed from the bird without harm to the bird.

3. Section 10 of the same Act deals with licensing matters. There is provision for the Government to grant licences to take birds for avicultural purposes but such licenses are not freely given and are confined generally to those species not readily obtainable from captive stock and, in addition, there are special restrictions on the methods which may be used for capture. They are not applicable in cases of commercial involvement.

BIRD PROTECTION

The Act mentioned lists the birds which may or may not be taken and these are listed under a series of schedules which are reproduced below. Particular attention should be paid to the **Fourth Schedule** which covers wild birds not to be sold alive unless close-ringed and bred in captivity.

First Schedule — Part 1

Wild birds and their eggs protected by special penalties **at all times**

Avocet	Grebe, black-necked
Bee-eater (all species)	Grebe, Slavonian
Bittern (all species)	Greenshank
Bluethroat	Gull, little
Brambling	Gull, Mediterranean
Bunting, Lapland	Harrier (all species)
Bunting, snow	Heron, purple
Buzzard, honey	Hobby
Chough	Hoopoe
Corncrake	Kingfisher
Crake, spotted	Kite
Crossbill	Merlin
Diver (all species)	Oriole, golden
Dotterel	Osprey
Eagle (all species)	Owl, barn
Falcon, gyr	Owl, snowy
Fieldfare	Peregrine
Firecrest	Phalarope, red-necked
Godwit, black-tailed	Plover, Kentish
Goshawk	Plover, little ringed

170

Quail, European
Redstart, black
Redwing
Rosefinch, scarlet
Ruff and reeve
Sandpiper, green
Sandpiper, wood
Serin
Shorelark
Shrike, red-backed
Sparrowhawk
Spoonbill
Stilt, black-winged
Stint, Temminck's

Stone curlew
Swan, whooper
Tern, black
Tern, little
Tern, roseate
Tit, bearded
Tit, crested
Treecreeper, short-toed
Warbler, Cetti's
Warbler, Dartford
Warbler, marsh
Warbler, Savi's
Woodlark
Wryneck

First Schedule — Part II

Wild birds and their eggs protected by special penalties **during the close season** 1st February to 31st August but which may be killed or taken at other times.

Whimbrel
Wild duck of the following species have the same close season except that in or over any area below high water mark the close season runs from 21st February to 31st August.

Common scoter
Garganey
Goldeneye

Long-tailed duck
Pintail
Scaup

Velvet scoter

Second Schedule

Wild birds which may be killed or taken by authorised persons.

Bullfinch
Cormorant
Crow, carrion
Crow, hooded
Domestic pigeon (gone feral)
Dove, collared
Goosander (Scotland only)
Gull, great black-backed
Gull, lesser black-backed
Gull, herring
Jackdaw
Jay
Magpie

Merganser, red-
breasted
(Scotland only)
Oystercatcher (only in certain areas)
Raven (Argyll and Skye only)
Rock dove (Scotland only)
Rook
Shag
Sparrow, house
Starling
Stock dove
Woodpigeon

171

Bullfinches are added to the Second Schedule in the administrative counties of Bedfordshire, Berkshire, Buckinghamshire, Cambridgeshire and the Isle of Ely; in Cornwall, the boroughs of Launceston, Saltash, the urban district of Torpoint and the rural districts of Launceston and St. Germans only; in Derby, the county borough of Derby, the urban district of Swadlincote and the rural districs of Shardlow and Repton only; in Devon, the county boroughs of Exeter, Plymouth and Torbay, the urban districts of Ashburton, Buckfastleigh, Budleigh Salterton, Dawlish, Exmouth, Kingsbridge, Newton Abbot, Salcombe, Tavistock and Teignmouth and the rural districts of Broadwoodwidger, Kingsbridge, Newton Abbot, Plympton St. Mary, St. Thomas, Tavistock and Totnes only; in Dorset, the rural district of Wimborne and Cranborne only; Essex including the county borough of Southend-on-Sea; in Gloucestershire, the borough of Tewkesbury and the rural districts of Cheltenham, Newent and North Cotswold only; Hampshire, Herefordshire, Hertfordshire, Huntingdonshire, Kent including the county borough of Canterbury; in the London boroughs of Croydon and that part of Newham which formerly comprised the county borough of East Ham only. Norfolk including the county borough of Norwich; in Oxfordshire the rural districts of Bullingdon and Henley only; in Rutland the rural district of Uppingham only; East and West Suffolk, Surrey, East Sussex including the county boroughs of Eastbourne, West Sussex; in Warwickshire the borough of Stratford-upon-Avon, Shipston-on-Stour and Alcester only; Worcestershire including the county boroughs of Dudley and Worcester. In all other areas the bullfinch is protected.

Any species not mentioned in the First, Second or Third Schedules, or in the Statutory Instruments, is fully protected throughout the year.

Third Schedule

Wild birds which may be killed or taken **outside the close season**, 1st February to 31st August except where indicated otherwise.

Note that the close season for wild duck and geese when below high water mark is 21st February to 31st August.

172

Those birds already shown in Part II of the First Schedule.

Capercaillie — close season 1st February to 30th September

Coot	Moorhen
Curlew (other than stone Curlew)	Plover, golden
	Plover grey
Gannet (on Sula Sgeir only)	Redshank, common
Godwit, bar-tailed	

Snipe, common — close season 1st February to 11th August
Snipe, jack — close season 1st February to 11th August

Wild duck of the following species (see note above)

Bean goose	Pink-footed goose
Canada goose	White-fronted goose
Greylag goose	

Woodcock — close season 1st February to 30th September except in Scotland where 1st February to 31st August.

Fourth Schedule

Wild birds which may **not** be sold alive unless close-ringed and bred in captivity:

Blackbird	Falcon, gyr	Kite, black
Blackcap	Falcon, red-footed	Kite, red
Bluethroat	Fieldfare	Lark (all species)
Brambling	Firecrest	Linnet
Bullfinch	Flycatcher (all species)	Magpie
Buntings (all species)		Martin (all species)
Buzzard, common	Goldcrest	Merlin
Buzzard, honey	Goldfinch	Nightingale
Buzzard, rough-legged	Goshawk	Nightjar
Chaffinch	Greenfinch	Nuthatch
Chiffchaff	Harrier, hen	Oriole, golden
Chough	Harrier, marsh	Osprey
Crossbill (all species)	Harrier, Montagu's	Owl (all species)
	Hawfinch	Peregrine
Cuckoo	Hobby	Pipit (all species)
Dipper	Hoopoe	Raven
Eagle, golden	Jay	Redpoll (all species)
Eagle, white-tailed	Kestrel, common	Redstart (all species)
	Kestrel, lesser	Redwing
	Kingfisher	Ring Ouzel

173

CAGE BIRD HYBRIDS

Robin
Shrike (all speices)
Siskin
Sparrow, hedge
Sparrow, house
Sparrow, tree
Sparrowhawk
Starling
Stonechat
Swallow

Thrush (all species)
Tit (all species,
   including bearded
   tit)
Treecreeper
Twite
Wagtail (all species)
Warbler (all species)
Waxwing
Wheatear

Whinchat
Whitethroat (all
  species)
Woodpecker (all
  species)
Wren
Wryneck
Yellowhammer

INDEX